HARD-HITTING STRATEGIES
UP TO BIGOTRY, MANAGING
PRODUCES, AND UTILIZIN
THAT GAY AND LESBIAN I
TO CREATE CHANGE

From singer Melissa Etheridge to Olympic champion
Greg Louganis, from tennis great Martina Navratilova to
the British actor Sir Ian McKellan, celebrities and nota-
bles have come forward to put a new face on gay and lesbian sexuality. At the same time, the religious right
campaigns to legalize discrimination against gays and promote an anti-gay prejudice in the general public. The result: cultural attitudes on this topic have never been so
polarized—or so openly discussed. The battle is on!

With all of this new visibility, tensions between gay people, their families, coworkers, and others have come out in
the open as never before. In *Setting Them Straight*, experienced therapist Dr. Betty Berzon, author of the classic
bestseller *Permanent Partners*, provides a unique battle
plan for confronting discrimination, whether it comes
from strangers or beloved friends and family. Understanding why people hate, the origins of prejudice, how to
channel anger, the answers to the rhetoric of bigotry, and
how to prevail in homophobic encounters are all a part of
Dr. Berzon's discussion. This book is a timely, important,
and much needed resource for a community under siege.

BETTY BERZON, PH.D., is a longtime psychotherapist and
activist. She is the author of the gay and lesbian self-help
classic *Permanent Partners* and the editor of *Positively Gay*.
She lives and practices in Los Angeles.

Also by Betty Berzon

Permanent Partners
Positively Gay

BETTY BERZON, PH.D.

author of permanent partners

SETTING THEM STRAIGHT

You CAN do something about bigotry and homophobia in your life

A PLUME BOOK

PLUME
Published by the Penguin Group
Penguin Books USA Inc., 375 Hudson Street, New York, New York 10014, U.S.A.
Penguin Books Ltd, 27 Wrights Lane, London W8 5TZ, England
Penguin Books Australia Ltd, Ringwood, Victoria, Australia
Penguin Books Canada Ltd, 10 Alcorn Avenue, Toronto, Ontario, Canada M4V 3B2
Penguin Books (N.Z.) Ltd, 182–190 Wairau Road, Auckland 10, New Zealand

Penguin Books Ltd, Registered Offices:
Harmondsworth, Middlesex, England

First published by Plume, an imprint of Dutton Signet,
a division of Penguin Books USA Inc.

First Printing, June, 1996
10 9 8 7 6 5 4 3 2 1

 REGISTERED TRADEMARK—MARCA REGISTRADA

LIBRARY OF CONGRESS CATALOGING-IN-PUBLICATION DATA
Berzon, Betty.
    Setting them straight : you can do something about bigotry and homophobia in
your life / Betty Berzon.
    p. cm.
    Includes bibliographical references and index.
    ISBN 0-452-27421-4
    1. Homophobia—United States. 2. Toleration—United States. 3. Hate—United
States. 4. Gay men—United States—Social conditions. 5. Lesbians—United States—
Social conditions. I. Title.
HQ76.3.U5B48   1996
305.9'0664—dc20   95-53214
                                                                                    CIP

Printed in the United States of America
Set in Transitional 521
Designed by Jesse Cohen

To Teresa DeCrescenzo
For All the Same Right Reasons

Acknowledgments

My thanks to the members of Project Angel Heart in Denver, Colorado, where the inspiration for this effort was first born.

To my friend, Paul Monette, who helped me understand that anger in the service of self-esteem is at the core of gay and lesbian empowerment.

To Jed Mattes, my agent, for his Lamaze-like coaching with this book that enabled it to get delivered into the world.

To Carole DeSanti, my editor, who was right about all those changes.

To Peter Nardi for his counsel early on.

To Terry DeCrescenzo, my loving partner, who makes it possible for me to write and to be a mensch, even when I don't want to be.

Table of Contents

Introduction

The seed for this book was planted one day when I was giving a talk to members of the gay and lesbian community of Denver, Colorado. It was just months before the disastrous 1992 election in which discrimination against gay people in Colorado was *legalized* by the passage of Amendment Two. Fear and disbelief were the prevailing reactions in that community—could this actually be happening twenty-three years after Stonewall?

To most people, the fact that the amendment was even on the ballot was surreal. Others were immersed in the reality of mounting a fight against this outrage, running scared but walking proud—going door to door to educate the citizenry as to what a yes vote on Amendment Two would mean.

On that day in Denver, a young man in the audience hesitantly held up his hand, and when I called on him he spoke in a voice so soft that I had to strain to hear him.

"I have this problem," he stammered. "When I hear some guy on television saying that I have chosen a lifestyle that is vile and disgusting, that I am a sick and disordered pervert, I just want to scream. I want to hurl myself into the television and rip his throat out. I feel so out of control I frighten myself. What do you do when that happens? What do *you* do?"

Heads were nodding throughout the audience as people turned to one another, then all eyes were on me—silence in the room, waiting for the answer.

"I feel the same way you do," I said.

The words hung in the air for a moment, then titters, and laughter swept through the audience. I wasn't sure why they were laughing. Did they think I was trivializing the young man's remarks by making a joke they should laugh at? I hadn't meant to be funny. Actually, I was dead serious. Looking back, I decided they had laughed out of the tension they felt on hearing that I was no more competent to deal with my anger than they were, that we all were frightened by the rage that mindless bigotry touches off in us.

I went away fretting that these people deserved a better response than I'd given them. I thought about it for weeks. I could have encouraged their activism, but these Colorado gays and lesbians were up to their ears in activism already. I could have suggested they use anger to add force to their campaign, but what I sensed was that most of them were so freaked out by what was happening that fear overshadowed anger.

The juxtapositioning of these two emotions—fear and anger—is what most often immobilizes us when we are confronted by someone's bigoted actions toward us. What are we so afraid of? These people are only as powerful as we allow them to be. The schoolyard bullies succeed because their illusion of power is made possible by their victims' illusion of powerlessness. Once the victims fight back the equation shifts.

I believe this illusion of powerlessness for most people begins in childhood (when we *are* truly without power) and is carried forward by any condition in one's adult life that transmits the message "You are less than."

Among the many circumstances that this message might refer to, there is the pervasive influence of being classified as a member of a discredited minority. Not many people are out there saying "What a wonderful thing to be gay or lesbian. How proud you must be to be a member of such an admired and distinguished part of the population, one held in such high esteem."

The message we do get is "How unfortunate you are to be less than all right." If you internalize that message, as many of us have done earlier in our lives, you might well believe that they *are* right and you aren't. You put yourself one down to *them*, allowing them a power over you that has no real basis in fact because you are just as all right as they are. The illusion of powerlessness wins over the reality of the *unused* power that too many gay and lesbian people live with.

I have seen this process in action in a variety of situations and with all kinds of people. Probably you have too. What would it take, I have asked myself, to convince ordinary gay men and lesbians of the power they have to challenge not only instances of overt bigotry, but the more subtle covert discrimination that often permeates our relationships with non-gay people, even those who love us? Is there some form of consciousness-raising–cum–assertiveness training needed here?

Or, could I possibly, in a book, inspire the confidence, provide the guidance, even suggest the words to use in encounters with homophobic people, from the worst bigots intent on annihilating our community to your old Aunt Mildred who is just trying to save your soul? This book is my attempt to inspire your willingness to put fear behind you and confront discrimination whenever you find it in your life.

One thing to bear in mind is that, for many people, their sense of reality is compromised when the rules change. Someone wrote that the current confrontation with the gay issue that the country is being subjected to is similar to what a family often goes through on learning that one of their own is gay or lesbian. There might be shock, anger, fear, hostility, and hysteria before there is understanding and acceptance.

One can hardly open a magazine or newspaper, or turn on

television these days without seeing something about gay. People who would have preferred not to deal at all with the lives of gays and lesbians presently have little choice. We are part of the business of America now, whether anybody likes it or not. For many, this is a drastic change and they don't quite know what to do with it—what is it okay to say or even think about homosexuality now that the rules are changing?

A dramatic public example of this occurred in the United States Congress when Representative Richard Armey, on the floor of the House of Representatives, referred to openly gay colleague Barney Frank as "Barney Fag." A great hue and cry went up—newspaper editorials, television commentators, government officials all condemning Armey for expressing his homophobic thought.

Armey claimed that he did not mean his remark as an insult. It was only a slip of the tongue, he said but he publicly apologized. The point was demonstrated. On the surface anyway, derogatory name-calling of gay people in a public forum is not something you can get away with in today's world.

A parallel dilemma regarding changing rules is that of the men in present-day society, most of whom grew up believing that women are on earth to please them, serve them, satisfy their sexual urges, and affirm their masculinity. These men were taught that women want to be seduced, that "no" really means "yes, but try a little harder," that women are flattered by any attention paid them by a man.

Then came the rude awakening. In what must have felt to many men like an overnight switch, the most benign-seeming overtures to females became grounds for legal action, and the presumed male prerogative of handling a woman's body at will could land a man in prison. The rules changed, and what had been accepted as routine behavior toward women was now sexual harassment and carried serious penalties.

Homophobia, and sexism, and sexual harassment all have one thing in common. The real issue is power—who has it and who doesn't. Our society has developed mainly around the needs of men, in whom most of the power has been vested. One important way of expressing male power has been the subjugation of women. That may or may not have appeared to be consensual before, but it surely is not now. Women have taken power of their own and, for the most part, no longer serve as society's handmaidens. Certain men resent this and act out their resentment in sometimes brutal ways.

Heterosexuals as a group have always had more power than homosexuals. We were subjugated by ridicule, disdain, and marginalization. Now gay and lesbian people are beginning to claim power through visibility in politics, and in the media. As gay and lesbian people begin to impose new rules for how we are willing to be treated, the power balance shifts.

Homophobic straights have to abandon some of their ways of exerting control over us. They are not giving up easily. Most do not understand that the assertion, or at least the illusion, of power is the driving force behind their bigotry, and the diminution of their ability to control our lives has caused them to increase their efforts to put limits on our freedom.

So, what does all this mean for our dealings with those who out of ignorance, frustration, orthodoxy, or malice strive to dishonor our existence? Should we be understanding of the underlying reasons for their homophobia? Of course, but only to know better how to neutralize their effect on us. In a given instance, acknowledging how hard it is to change one's beliefs might even be the best strategy for being heard in a homophobic encounter.

I am not so naive as to think that the suggestions I am making here will have the effect of eliminating someone's entrenched bigotry, though I'd like to think that could happen. Our best chances to change anyone's mind and heart are with those people who simply don't have accurate information about who we are, and don't understand the emotional needs served by their own prejudices.

Speaking up, and talking back to bigotry repositions us more effectively on the social landscape and challenges the assumption that gay and lesbian people are willing to be sitting ducks for anyone who thinks he or she has permission to condemn us.

Not unimportant is the personal payoff that facing up to discrimination can offer. To *not* absorb antigay messages, but instead to stand up for yourself, and represent the truth reinforces your sense of yourself as a person who *can* effect change. Being gay or lesbian is an essential element in your identity. Taking action to validate that element, you operate from the center of your being, defying anyone's attempts to reinvent you as a deserving target of their animosity.

When I encounter someone's antigay bigotry, his or her words have a hollow ring to them. There is nothing inside me cued to receive those messages. I know who I am, what I am about, where I have been, and why that person is behaving irrationally. I know because I have been where that person is.

In the years when I was fooling myself into believing that I was heterosexual, I felt antagonism toward gay people. I did not realize that I was rejecting an important part of myself. I just thought those homosexual people were all wrong and I didn't want them around me. I let them know that, and some were puzzled by my actions since I was otherwise an open, liberal person.

Those who weren't puzzled were the lesbians who saw right through my charade, who understood that I was behaving irrationally to protect myself, to hold the truth at bay. When I finally was able to see this for myself, to accept my own lesbian identity, I didn't need to discriminate against homosexuals anymore. I was okay, they were okay, we were okay.

What really made an essential difference was when *I* learned to speak as the gay person I was. At first it was frightening because for so many years I had feared I would be destroyed if I exposed my secret, the part of me that was so vulnerable to what people thought.

But then I met others who had moved beyond that point— gay and lesbian activists who were challenging the status quo, redefining the rules—and they became my models for how to talk back to prejudice and discrimination. I borrowed from their courage and put myself into the action. I brought the disparate parts of my being into a kind of unity. It is the best thing I've ever done for myself.

One thing about all this is clear. It's time to stop defending our gay and lesbian lives and begin confronting the bigotry without which homosexuality *would not be an issue*. We must combat ignorance and keep the pressure on the American public to understand us.

We must arm ourselves with information about why people are prejudiced and the psychological payoff of scapegoating strangers. We must use this knowledge to fight intolerance and injustice, even those small instances where you know the person does not mean to injure you but you come away nursing a wound anyway. I say "we" must do these things. I am talking about me, and you.

The problem is that this is an imperfect scenario. You probably do not think of yourself as a combatant. You just want to be left alone to live your life. You want to be liked, respected, and accepted as you are. Nowhere in *this* scenario is there motivation to be engaged in conflict, or be a fighter in the struggle to change the way an entire class of people is treated. That is understandable and reasonable. What it is not is *realistic*.

But maybe you want something in between being a combatant and being left alone. You want to be involved, be part of the changing world, engaged and active, but you don't know how to come to that. You believe you might have a contribution to make, but where in yourself do you find the motivation to implement that belief? You may even have the information you need about the practicalities—whom to call, which organization seems appropriate—but somehow you can't seem to take the step.

First you have to deal with whatever is stopping you from joining the action. Is it fear of doing something different from what you have ever done before? Is it fear of possibly being unable to rise to the action? Are you scared of what the fallout would be in your personal life?

All of these fears are recognizable to me. I certainly have felt them. Most people who go into activism of any kind, at any level, do so feeling some trepidation about their ability to carry through, and the consequences to their personal welfare.

The important thing is that they do it anyway. They take the next step—make appearances, lend their voice to a protest, communicate their feelings about an issue. You are not alone when you feel afraid. You are not alone when you put fear behind you and act. Overcoming your fears to act on your beliefs can feel very satisfying. It is a triumph of the will.

The problem is if gay and lesbian people do not take responsibility for changing how we are treated by the larger society, who will? What must *sometimes* be sacrificed in taking such a stand is the need to be liked—to be the one who fits in, doesn't make waves, is reliably pleasant, and never calls the question on someone else's irrational behavior, no matter how hurtful it is.

I realize that this is easier said than done, that a lifetime of being a person who puts courtesy and consideration first is not transformed by the first clarion call to action. But the need is not to reconstruct your personality, it is for you to be willing, on occasion, to forgo the fear in order to fight antigay bigotry, whether it's subtle and denied, or blatant and proudly owned.

You and I are diminished by discrimination when the value of our very existence is questioned. When we don't respond, when we don't fight back, our integrity as gay and lesbian human beings is further compromised. Talking back to bigotry is posing the issue of our right to love versus their right to hate. The verdict hangs on how willing we are to stand up to the homophobia in our own lives.

I have written here about why it is so hard for most of us to overcome the fear of coming out and speaking out, and what can be done to rise above that fear. By way of example, I offer scenarios of the private encounters with homophobia that any of us might have to deal with in our everyday life.

I have also presented variations on the theme—ways to fight bigotry that don't involve direct confrontation, including stories of successful efforts to educate and inform, raise consciousness, and use the processes of democracy to improve the gay and lesbian experience in the workplace.

Because knowing what makes an opponent "tick" always helps in an adversarial encounter, I have written what we know about why people hate, what prejudice is, the reasons behind scapegoating, and the difference between true morality and the religious right's version. I've also dealt with the issue of anger, how to understand and manage it when it boils over in the presence of antigay bigotry.

In the hope that all this has brought you to the brink of encounter, there are three chapters here on the typical issues that homophobic people bring up, and what to say in response. I have also written about "going public"—those opportunities to educate regarding gay and lesbian issues through radio and television appearances and participation in other public forums. I'd like to think that what I have provided will help to make you an effective adversary in all of these encounters. That is the challenge of this book.

Part I——Defining the Problem

1

Antigay Bigotry and You

You are a gay man sitting at your desk in the office where you work and two of your associates walk by. One is telling the other a "fag" joke. Both laugh uproariously at the tag line. You can feel the heat rising in your face as you stare down at the papers you're working on.

You are a lesbian getting an estimate on repairing some damage to your home from a water leak. The contractor hands you his paperwork and suggests that you probably will want your husband to look this over. You watch him going out the door while you're still deciding whether to inform him that you are a lesbian and quite capable of dealing with his estimate on your own.

You are in an airport and you overhear a nearby group of men hashing over a court case that's in the news. The defendant has just been given probation for bashing a gay man he didn't know. The group agrees that the defendant should have been acquitted since the damn fairy probably brought it on himself by hitting on this poor guy because that's what fairies do. You glare at the group but they don't even know you're there.

You are visiting your family with whom you have never shared that you are gay. Someone at the dinner table tells a story ridiculing a co-worker who is blatantly homosexual and effeminate and the whole table giggles about it. You feel as if you want to scream at them but you just go right on eating.

These are the kinds of situations most of us have been through time and again. The common thread is the impotence we feel as we are faced with the dilemma of what, if anything, we should say or do. What do we feel? Anger? Fear? Confusion? How do we decide whether to act or not? What will the consequences be if we do? Is this person important enough to us to avoid risking rejection? What is the priority here? Just to stay out of trouble? Just to get the job done? Just to cooperate with the prevailing mood?

And how many times have you come away from situations such as those described above wanting to kick yourself because you were unable to speak up, didn't know what to say, or were too intimidated by the thought of what the fallout might be to do anything? If your answer is often, you have a lot of company.

The problem is, until we begin to confront the kind of ignorance and bigotry involved in these encounters, they will go on reinforcing the assumptions of heterosexuality, the antigay stereotypes, and the discrimination that negatively affects the life of every gay and lesbian person, whether we are direct targets of that discrimination or not.

Defining Discrimination in Your Life

How do you know when you are being discriminated against? If someone swings a baseball bat in your direction while shouting antigay invectives, you can be pretty sure you are the target of a homophobic attack. If someone refuses to serve "your kind" in a public establishment, you are clearly being discriminated against. When you are passed over for a promotion and it is evident that it is because you are known to be gay, you are the victim of bigotry.

But if nothing like this has ever happened to you, you may feel that discrimination is not much of a factor in your life. You don't encounter hostile bigots. You have never been chased down the street by crazed teenagers, refused service in a restaurant, or deprived of job advancement because of your sexual orientation.

You live a well-ordered life. You do not call undue attention to being gay or lesbian. You are law-abiding, discreet, not a troublemaker, and you give no one reason to discriminate against you. The trouble is, they don't need a reason.

When the religious right promotes antigay ballot initiatives, it doesn't matter where it is happening. If you are gay or lesbian, it's about *your* potential to move freely in this society and enjoy the same rights and privileges that nongay citizens enjoy.

When a television program does a story on gay and lesbian parenting and included is a condemnation of gays as parents by homophobically obsessed psychologist Joseph Nicolosi, it is *your* right and worthiness to be a parent that he is condemning. When highly placed public officials attack the decency and integrity of gays and lesbians in the military, it is an attack on the decency and integrity of every gay or lesbian person.

When they scorn homosexuals as aberrant and predatory, they are scorning you. When the Vatican issues a document saying that it is legitimate to discriminate against homosexuals in employment, housing, and the adoption of children, they are talking about you.

This kind of discrimination has nothing to do with how carefully you live your life, what a nice person you are, or how much you contribute to the United Way. You cannot earn immunity from bigotry, though sometimes you can create the illusion for yourself that you are doing that.

This illusion is commonly seen in the relationships many gay people have with their families. There evolves a conspiracy of silence around the word *gay*. The conspiracy turns on the unspoken agreement that, if we never say the word, we don't have to deal with the reality. For this "magical thinking" to be maintained, certain acts of subterfuge and surrender are required.

For instance, you must "put away" the telltale magazines and books when the folks come to visit. Your lover becomes your "friend" at cousin Sally's wedding. You make a joke when asked by relatives about your prospects for marriage. You avoid the social events your co-workers enjoy together. You sanitize accounts of your activities off the job. You allow the hotel clerk to insist on twin beds for you and your lover, then spend half an hour rearranging the furniture in the hotel room.

You may not think any of this is a big deal. You are so used to these ways of coping. It's a familiar routine, regularly occurring, often subtle enough to ignore. But it is these subtle instances of discrimination—of living with the effects of homophobia without protest—that reinforce the notion that gay and lesbian people have few choices when it comes to dealing with bigotry, that you are stuck with the ignorance and intolerance of the homophobic people in your life.

The fact is that you are not stuck, you have a number of options to fight discrimination. Of course, you do have to acknowledge that it's happening to you, first.

Standing up to Bigotry Means Coming Out Again . . . and Again

Wherever you are in your coming-out process, you probably know by now that it is a story without end. Every new person you encounter has to be dealt with in terms of you being gay or lesbian, even if you choose to deal with him or her by ignoring the subject. *That* is a coming-out decision in itself.

Deciding to fight back against bigotry in your own life is a giant step in the coming-out process. It will take you further out of the closet than you have been before, and it will be the most self-validating thing you have ever done as a gay or lesbian person.

There is a natural inclination in human beings to become known to those in our lives who mean the most to us. That inclination drives us to disclose ourselves so that we may experience human connectedness and closeness. We tend to matter to those who know us best so we are inclined to make ourselves known to the people around us.

The dilemma for gays and lesbians is that these folks we care so much about and want to disclose to are often the same people with whom we have the most apprehension when it comes to revealing that we are gay. They are also the people we find it difficult to confront when their homophobia is the issue that inhibits our becoming known to them. With people close to us, especially family, it can feel as if there is too much at stake to risk rejection or abandonment through disclosure.

For example, I have known prominent gay and lesbian activists who have never told certain members of their family that they are gay. These activists are people who talk openly about being gay to large audiences of strangers, whose lives are shaped by their dedicated community work, who personally lobby highly placed elected officials on behalf of gay and lesbian causes, but who behave as if they are in shark-infested waters with certain relatives when it comes to disclosing that they are gay. What is going on here?

The difference is that speaking publicly, creating community, lobbying politicians is *empowering* business. When you are confronted with a (possibly) homophobic relative, you come to the task unprotected by the activist's anger or the debater's detachment.

With Aunt Mildred, you are not "psyched" to meet an opponent whose bigotry is established and toward whom you have given yourself permission to be angry. Neither are you approaching a situation in which everyone knows the rules and the emphasis is on substance and style. You are just there with Aunt Mildred who you *suspect* is homophobic, toward whom you are not angry (yet), and there are no rules.

In the power equation between you and your relative, you may perceive yourself to be on the losing end—once again the child seeking the powerful adult's approval. If you have tasted the honey of speaking freely about being gay and of being unapologetic about who you are, it is distasteful to have to backslide into deceit. Most likely, you will just avoid that relative, and the intimidating power equation remains the same in your mind because you have made no effort to change it.

Is the fear of possible loss—social approval, financial gain, family loyalty—so great that people will go to any lengths to avoid it? The answer is yes for many who have not discovered that the more enduring source of self-esteem for anyone gay or lesbian is the freedom to be authentically who and what we are, anytime, anywhere, and with anyone.

The problem is that too many people won't risk disclosure because of their lifelong exposure to the antigay messages that are everywhere in this society—church, school, media, their own families. These negative messages get internalized and can inhibit any inclination to explore the real risks of coming out. Again, the power imbalance between gay or lesbian people and others in their world remains the same because there has been no attempt to change it.

The reality is that there are all kinds of people out there. A great many nongay people couldn't care less about your homosexuality. Either they are people who had no such prejudice to start with because of the kind of family they grew up in, or who have been able to rise above their prejudices because they are sufficiently educated and sophisticated, or they are just so secure in their own identity that they are not threatened by people who are different from them.

On the other hand, there are people who are eager to tell you what's wrong with your gay or lesbian life and why you should be ashamed. These "critics" are not all right-wing extremists either. Some are ordinary, decent folk who are just following the crowd, without deliberate malice or conscious intent to injure. Their prejudices are fixed and they have never had reason to question them. They resent being called bigots; they see themselves as simply adhering to a belief system that is commonly shared. They're fine, you're not, and that stays the same for them, and for you, until something happens to change it.

So how do you tell the difference between the person who really does pose a threat, and the person whose acceptance you don't need to *earn*? The answer is, you can't make that distinction consistently. Can you tell by looking at someone that he or she hates homosexuals? If you know where someone is from, or what his or her work is, do you know how that person feels about gay people? You may think you know, but you could be wrong as easily as you could be right.

Depending on stereotypes is risky business—your sister's macho boyfriend probably hates fags, your mother's religious friend is undoubtedly homophobic, the new neighbor down the street has beady eyes and looks like a bigot. You could be wrong on some, or even all of these counts. Who knows better than gay and lesbian people how unreliable stereotypes are for conveying a truth about someone?

The trouble with deciding a priori that people are hostile to who you are is that it reinforces the *reluctance* to be honest in dealing with them. The assumption of animosity justifies steering clear of certain individuals, in your family, at work, at school, in the community. Once again, nothing changes in the power equation.

Why are we so afraid to find out who is friend and who is foe? Why are we so inclined to avoid confrontation with those in our lives who are homophobic—the dedicated bigots as well as our well-intentioned friends and relatives? I think there are two major reasons.

First, we have all looked into the fun-house mirror of anti-gay prejudice and seen the distorted image that is reflected back to us. In addition to the distorted image we must cope with, it is almost impossible for any gay or lesbian person growing up in this society not to have swallowed some of the toxins of antigay bigotry—the assertions that being gay or lesbian is sick, depraved, degenerate, and an abomination to God. The message to gay people is "hate yourself," and many of us have had to struggle not to accede to that message.

One of the worst effects that the antigay toxins work on us are those feelings of doubt when we suspect, however momentarily, that they might be right about us. It is in those moments that we might give in to fear and apathy, when it seems we have no defense against our detractors who have righteous truth on their side: Are we not the frivolous, sex-obsessed, party-going adolescents they say we are? Don't we trivialize our intimate relationships, preferring variety to constancy?

How easy it is to slip into this homophobic thinking, and intimidate ourselves. Yes, some of us are frivolous and sex-obsessed, some of us are not yet ready for long-term relationships, but most of us are just as eager to have and hold on to our partnerships, live serious and productive lives, and enjoy sex as an expression of love with one person as our heterosexual counterparts are.

The second reason for avoiding confrontation with homophobia is the wish that most people have to live a life that is reasonably trouble-free. The last thing in the world you want to do is to *invite* conflict. You'll settle for being liked and respected. You'd prefer to be loved and admired.

You have had plenty of evidence that challenging someone's beliefs does not usually bring you his or her gratitude, much less his or her love and admiration. So you keep the lid on those opinions, feelings, and reactions that might create conflict with others. The problem here is that you are essentially keeping the lid on *you*.

Any time you avoid being honest about who you really are—about something so central to your being as the social, emotional, and psychological aspects of being gay or lesbian—you are relating to others with only a part of yourself. The rest is lost to understanding, to respect, to real love.

And, for the purposes to which this book is dedicated, you are lost to the battle against bigotry that is the best hope for those of us who are gay and lesbian to be wholly understood, wholly respected, and wholly loved.

But I will assume that since you *are* reading this book, you are a person who wants to make changes in yourself and in your society. There is something appealing to you about taking a further step out of the closet—this opportunity to be more than an innocent bystander to history.

More important, perhaps, you see a chance here to influence the forces in your own life that can, at times, cause you to feel disparaged and stigmatized. Fighting antigay prejudice puts *you* in charge of defining your own identity. You set the rules for how you are treated.

Of course, it is important for all of us to acknowledge that we are sometimes afraid of the changes that could occur in our lives if we become a person who confronts bigotry and demands equal time for the truth. But it is also important to give ourselves the gift of opportunity—to test our strength and courage, to find out, as Walt Whitman wrote, "I am larger, better than I thought. I did not know I held so much goodness."

The Messages We Give Ourselves

We all carry on inner dialogues with ourselves at some level of consciousness. We give ourselves messages about what is happening, what will be happening, and the roles those around us are playing, or will play, in the dramas of our daily lives.

As a psychotherapist, I work with the messages that people give themselves about themselves. I listen for repetition:

"I don't understand what is happening."

"I can't make anything work in my life."

"I know I'm not going to like this."

"I can't change."

Of equal importance are the messages people give themselves about others in their life:

"He wants me to be miserable."

"She doesn't care about me."

"He just wants to control me."

"I can't trust her."

"He's all wrong for me."

Of course, there is a purpose for the person behind every one of these messages. Sometimes the purpose is to stay in a fog about one's own responsibility for what is happening. Sometimes it is to avoid the demands of growing intimacy, or to avoid the vulnerability of feeling anything. Sometimes the purpose is to resist progress, the pain of failure being too familiar a companion to give up. Sometimes it is just an excuse not to try.

I have also become accustomed to listening to the messages that gay and lesbian people give themselves when faced with a personal experience of homophobia:

"There's no use talking to these people."

"I'm too angry to respond."

"It's too dangerous for me to get involved."

"I hate confrontation."

The purpose of all these messages is to *convince* one's self that it's okay not to get into a confrontation with bigotry, even if it means living with the hurt, anger, fear, and disillusionment that homophobic encounters can produce. If you have had such experiences, you know how frustrating it is to be the target of discrimination and be convinced (having convinced yourself) that you can't really do anything about it. That is perhaps the most frequent message we gay and lesbian people give ourselves in the face of intolerance:

"I can't do anything about it, because (fill in the blank)."

I understand that experience. I have had it. I will probably have it again, but I think it is time for all of us to move beyond "I can't do anything about it." There's a lot we can do, starting with replacing the old self-inhibiting messages with new self-affirming ones:

"I'm going to face this challenge for my own self-esteem."

"I will channel my anger into assertiveness."

"It's too dangerous for me to *let* this go on."

"This is important enough to overcome my distaste for confrontation."

"I can and will do something about this."

The first step in replacing your self-inhibiting messages with self-affirming ones will be the determination to catch yourself anytime the message coming through is a version of:

"I can't do anything about it."

You must listen for the words that seem to get you off the hook when you are considering an action. The inner monologue must then become a dialogue—you talking back to yourself, protesting that you *are* going to do something different this time, whether your internal self-critic likes it or not.

Catching yourself won't be easy at first. You have probably been living with this inclination to play it safe for a long time. Society reinforces the message: Avoid conflict, go along to get along, don't make waves. But the time is over for gay people to be silent and invisible. The price for that silence is too high. The danger of remaining invisible is too great. That is true for the gay and lesbian community at large, and it is true for you, and for me.

Actually there are few more self-negating experiences than being silent in the face of discrimination. You become the child without a voice. But you personally do not want to be that child. You want to be heard, and seen, and paid attention to. You want to join the action, to be yourself, and assert some influence. The reward of stepping up to have your say is that you feel all the rightness and goodness that goes with being authentically who and what you are.

Taking Responsibility

I like an expression I heard in a speech given by Michael Denneny, the preeminent gay editor. Michael was talking about Richard Rouilard, former editor-in-chief of the *Advocate*, who was being honored by the National Gay and Lesbian Journalists' Association. Referring to Richard's decision to dedicate his career to working for the good of gay and lesbian people, Michael called it the "spontaneous assumption of responsibility."

I thought, "That's it, that's what we need from a great many people—the spontaneous assumption of responsibility for fighting bigotry." I'd like to believe that inside every gay and lesbian person there is an activist trying to get out. I cannot imagine that anyone gay who is the target of discrimination (all of us?) wouldn't like to be able to strike a telling blow to the irrational prejudice, unearned hostility, and dehumanizing agenda of those who oppose us. What would make that possible?

It usually takes a personal crisis for the ordinary citizen to make the transition to activism. The mother whose child is killed by a drunk driver starts an organization to crack down on drunk driving. A woman whose husband is shot in a presidential assassination attempt becomes a major activist for gun control. The reality of living our gay and lesbian lives under the persistent threat of assault by antigay bigots, or even well-intentioned but ignorant bystanders, ought to be personal crisis enough to inspire activism.

The best examples we have of this transition to activism are the courageous men and women in the U.S. armed forces who have come out as gay knowing it would jeopardize their military careers, possibly even their freedom. I am convinced that these are people who never planned to be activists, but who could not continue to be silent and invisible in the face of the injustices they and others in the service were enduring—gay men and lesbians whose only "crime" was their sexual orientation.

I have a fantasy in which every gay or lesbian person currently in the U.S. military resigns and enlists in the battle for gay and lesbian civil rights. I'd say to them, "They don't want you, we do. They don't want you to be openly gay, we do. We honor you for who you are. We need you. Come join us!" Just imagine what progress we could make with all that personpower, talent, expertise, and dedication!

In the meantime, the battle is ours to wage. Fighting homophobia is a necessity, whether it's in our families, in our communities, or in ourselves. It is a necessity because there is no other choice that works—hide, deny, disguise, turn away, run away—antigay bigotry continues to be in all our lives.

Certain people will feel free to hate us until we confront the irrationality of that hatred and demand accountability for the damage they cause us. Others will continue to misunderstand who we are and unmaliciously hurt us until we overcome our inhibitions and educate them to the truth.

Can that work? Is prejudice reversible? The social scientists tell us yes, if the appeal is appropriate to the needs of the person. Some who are prejudiced might respond to an intellectual/logical argument if being seen as reasonable is highly valued by them.

Some may respond to an emotional appeal if they see themselves as essentially caring people. Some may respond to a motivational appeal if approval, prestige, status, or financial gain is substituted for whatever payoff their prejudices offered.

Prejudice can be amenable to change, but the priority I am pushing here is not *necessarily* the transformation of the homophobic people in your life into loving supporters of your sexual identity. My priority is to help you to have an empowering experience by confronting discrimination with the truth. This may seem like a limited goal, but it is important to be realistic.

Until this society is better able to produce positive mental health in our citizens, people will continue to resort to maladaptive strategies for "being okay," like striking out at innocent individuals in order to feel strong and competent and good about themselves.

If I make it sound like the only option is to leap feet-first into the middle of the action, I do not mean to give that impression. Coming to terms with our fears, with the self-inhibiting messages we give ourselves, may need to happen slowly, a few steps at a time.

When I first became involved with gay activism it was a short time after I had come out to myself. I was fortunate enough to become a part of a group planning the Los Angeles Gay and Lesbian Community Services Center, which had not yet opened. My job was to train a cadre of young lesbians and gay men to lead growth groups at the new center. Their job, unbeknownst to me, was to raise my consciousness about being gay.

I would go out with my little troupe of activists to speak at universities and before organizations. They all told their stories of coming out and I acted as the moderator. Nearly always someone in the audience asked if I was gay. I dutifully answered, completely unaware that I skillfully talked all around the truth.

Finally, my young friends sat me down and informed me that I had three answers to the questions about being gay. One took fifteen minutes, one ten minutes, and one five minutes, and in none of these version did I *ever* say I *was* gay. I was astonished. They got me. I had to admit that I was still nervous about taking that step, though I had fooled myself into thinking I was being perfectly honest.

It took me awhile to replace my rambling nonanswer to a three-second "Yes, I am gay." It happened slowly because I was reversing forty years of denial. There is rarely change without conflict. Facing the conflict rather than running away from it is the first step toward allowing creative change in one's life.

A Caution

In any confrontation, it's important to "know when to hold 'em and when to fold 'em." On encountering someone who is just so recalcitrant, so rooted in his bigotry that it seems pointless to try to continue the dialogue, you'll know when to back off—when your patience is at an end, and your level of anger is beginning to choke you. Just remember, the failure is not in you but in the other person's inability to find his way out of the prison of his prejudice.

Guidelines

So, how do we go about this assault on bigotry? In later chapters you will find scenarios for situations that you might encounter, with acquaintances, strangers, neighbors, friends, relatives, or co-workers. You will also see how to deal with certain gay or lesbian persons who may not be aware of the homophobic nature of their own comments.

These scenarios have no resolution. They are simply intended to highlight issues relevant to the kind of person being encountered. They deal with the themes that predictably come up anytime homophobia is being expressed. As you put yourself in these scenes, you may feel that the directness expressed is more than you would be up to, the language used more well thought out than you would probably be able to produce in the moment.

Think of the dialogue in these scenes as a road map, not the actual terrain. If you couldn't be this straightforward, don't worry about it. If words do not flow so trippingly from your tongue, don't be bothered. It's the *direction* that the conversation takes that is most important.

Just hearing yourself speak the truth in response to someone else's distorted notions will be self-affirming. The willingness to engage at all is an act of courage—the pivotal importance of *not* opting out of the encounter, a reach beyond what was thought to be possible, the reward of believing in yourself.

2

The Anticipation of Angst— Rising above Expectations

Finding myself recently with an extra day to spend on a trip to St. Louis, where I was born and spent my childhood, I got a crazy idea. Actually, it seemed like such a crazy idea that I told several friends hoping they would talk me out of it. No, they all thought it sounded like a great adventure and insisted that I do it. With some trepidation I set the process in motion.

From the time I was in kindergarten until the seventh grade I hung out with the same five girls. We were a tight little group. All of us lived within a few blocks of one another in a neighborhood that might as well have been zoned Jewish Only. We were all alike, or so it seemed, and we were inseparable.

When I was twelve years old my asthma was getting worse. To avoid the brutal midwestern winter, the doctor prescribed the warm desert air of Arizona. Sad to leave my friends, I was bundled off to Tucson and a gentile world, where I felt for the first time in my life like an outsider. Gradually I adjusted, but always looking forward to returning to St. Louis and familiar ground. It never happened.

The desert air did agree with me, my asthma disappeared, and we stayed in Arizona until I finished high school. I went off to college in California and my family followed. St. Louis was over, and so were my relationships with the gang of five I'd been so close to. I never saw any of them again.

It is now more than fifty years later. My crazy idea is to try to get my gang together. Fifty-plus years since I've seen them!? Could I even find them? Would any of them care? What a crazy idea, but something inside me couldn't leave it alone. Okay, I'd try. What did I have to lose?

While still in Los Angeles, I called my St. Louis cousin who I knew had stayed in touch with one of these "girls." He thought a reunion was a terrific idea and he offered to call his friend, Joyce, to make sure she remembered who I was after five decades. He called back in a few minutes to say she did indeed remember and wanted to see me.

"Call her," he insisted, giving me her number. I waited. I was losing my nerve. Why did I want to do this? What was I letting myself in for? I decided I'd better do it immediately or I wouldn't do it at all. I called. The conversation went well and Joyce offered to contact the others and have a luncheon at her home. I was surprised to learn that all the surviving "girls" lived in St. Louis and were still in contact with one another.

After several phone calls the luncheon was set up. I heard that everyone was eager to see me. I wondered what they were expecting—not a lesbian activist, I wagered. What was I expecting? What kind of people would these twelve-year-olds have turned out to be? This could be a disaster. No, I had to tell myself to stop thinking that way. This was just a little adventure, an archaeological dig into the far-off past, not really that important in the general scheme of my life.

On the appointed day in St. Louis I felt anxious though I wasn't sure what the anxiety was about. A clue. I dressed carefully, not wanting to look too butch, something I could hardly do if I tried. I took a cab to Joyce's house. It was in an upscale enclave, big homes, perfect lawns, quiet, genteel, a little unreal.

I was greeted at the door by an older woman, expensively turned out; smiling, she threw her arms around me. My God, this was not an older woman. This was my old friend Sadie, and she was exactly the same age as I was.

Sadie led me into the living room and there they were, my gang, plus a few more. Seven women, all beautifully dressed, all my age, not a gray head in the bunch, most with the same soft blond color that gets applied to my own hair every few months. Diamonds as big as the Ritz adorned their well-kept hands. I had to look closely at those sixty-plus faces to find the twelve-year-olds I had left behind. Amazingly, I did find them.

Marcia, who as a child wore thick glasses that made her look as if she were perennially searching for something she'd lost. No sign of eyeglasses now. The other Marcia, my best friend, quietly exploring my face for signs of *her* little friend. Sadie, blond then and blond now, still a little raucous. Lois, tanned, svelte, sheathed in silk. Roz, the sister of Bernard, whom I had a crush on in the second grade. Henrietta, whom I remembered just slightly from the old neighborhood, and Joyce, small as she always was, sweet, warm, and a little airy.

I was greeted with enthusiasm and, later, was startled to hear all the details that they remembered about me. I felt at ease with these women, accepted, so far anyway. I brought out my copy of our fifth-grade class picture. Joyce produced her copy as well. Memories flooded back. I was revisiting my childhood. More important, I saw that I had given myself the chance to see who I would have been if I hadn't left St. Louis (which none of them ever did) and weren't a lesbian (which none of them were, I assumed).

We were seated at an elegant table and with the serving of lunch their stories began. All had married well, five of the seven were widowed. All had grandchildren. Only one went to college and then for just one year. The others married early because that's what nice Jewish girls did to please their families. There were obligatory obituaries of husbands for my benefit since they all knew one another's stories by heart.

They talked about their children and grandchildren, gossiped about a certain "bad girl" who got pregnant in high school, and delightedly assassinated the character of the only one of our gang who had died: Helen Mae, who married an "older man," became a wild person who stole things from stores, and alienated her children, who didn't even come to her funeral.

Fascinated by all this, I was also beginning to wonder where I came in, when Henrietta asked, "Betty, do you work?" My heart stopped for a moment. This was my opening. I took a deep breath and said that I was a psychologist and I worked exclusively with gay and lesbian people because I was gay myself. Forks paused in midair.

"Really?" someone said. "Yes," I answered, and I launched into the story of my life since the age of twelve. I was just getting into the gay part when Joyce left the table, returning in a few seconds holding a piece of kitchen equipment in her hand.

"Look, everybody, here's my electric bagel slicer." (This was in response to several comments that had been made about how unusually thin the bagels were sliced. It was also in response, I thought, to a certain tension she perceived as I talked about being a lesbian.) After a few ohs and ahs about the bagel slicer, heads turned toward me and I resumed my story, determined not to be deterred again.

I described fearing I was gay as an adolescent, fighting it as a young adult, coming to accept and value my gayness, and building a career around it. By now, everyone was listening raptly. From the questions they asked it was obvious I was talking about something that was essentially alien to their lives. I talked about my work in the gay and lesbian community, my lover, my life. I felt their interest and I was exhilarated.

Henrietta volunteered that two lovely women who were a couple lived next door to her. One of the Marcias said that she had a nephew who was gay. Another said her hairdresser was gay. And that seemed to sum up their experience with gay, at least what they were willing to talk about. More questions were asked. I went into detail about what life was like these days for most gay and lesbian people—the discrimination, the gay rights movement, the positive energy that comes from diverse people working together for the same goals.

Dessert was served. My companions went back briefly to their insular gossip, but interest had been piqued. Over coffee, they came back to me with more questions. I was pleased. I believed I had opened the door to my world for them and they were not afraid to at least peer in. When lunch was over we began our leave-taking. They all agreed that we should do this again next year when I came to St. Louis. Hugs and kisses all around.

When I got back to the hotel Joyce called. She said she wanted to apologize because no one really asked questions about my "friend." She didn't want me to think they weren't interested. I told her we could talk about that next year, or maybe I'd just bring her along. She thought that would be lovely.

I sat in my hotel room thinking that I had just done something wonderful. There were times in my life when, in a setting like that, I would have felt embarrassed to talk about being homosexual because I *was* embarrassed about it. I would have felt that I hadn't developed properly to where these grown-up women were.

Now I felt very different. My children are not my biological issue but I am proud of the guidance I've given to thousands of gay and lesbian young people struggling to achieve good and productive lives. My confidence and self-worth come not from successfully conforming to the expectations of family, but from creating family where there was none before.

So I had experienced the reality of these women's lives once so much like mine, and they had experienced the reality of my life, so different from theirs. I had given them the gift of my presence and the knowledge of my being. Whatever homophobic prejudices they came in with and went out with, they would have to think about *me* whenever they heard or thought anything about gay.

I laughed to myself. I suspected the telephone wires would soon be buzzing. Fifty-plus years of new material to talk about and a topic that I hoped would inspire discussion for some time to come.

This tying together of past and present had been easy once I got over my initial anxiety. What was I so anxious about, their knowing I was gay? But I had planned all the time to tell them. Was my nervousness about being reduced to a stereotype— not being given a chance to be all that I am? But I did, in fact, give them the opportunity to know me by talking freely about myself.

Had I censored, danced around my sexual orientation, presented a false picture in order to be accepted, I would have betrayed myself, and them. By simply letting them get to know me I offered a nonthreatening lesson in gay awareness they probably would never have encountered otherwise.

Speaking Openly about Your Life as a Gay or Lesbian Person—"Normalizing" to Counter Homophobia

Speaking casually, but honestly, about your life as if you *expect* the nongay person to be interested and accepting is a way of establishing a kind of "ground rule" for interaction with co-workers, relatives, friends, and strangers who are not gay. You may be aware that there is some antagonism to your sexual orientation, but you can defuse that by doing an end run around it, behaving as you would if there were not an element of homophobia involved.

"Yes, my lover (partner) and I went there on *our* vacation last year."

This is not confrontation and it is not an attempt to change anyone's core beliefs. It is simply a statement of fact that carries the message: I do not have to hide my life from you because there is nothing to hide. I do the same things you do because I am like you.

Too often, people anticipate discrimination and then proceed as though it were inevitable. It is not. While in some situations I believe it is useful to confront discrimination, there is also much to be accomplished by simply giving the other person a chance to know you. Surveys of nongays consistently tell us that knowing gay or lesbian people makes a significant difference in how they feel about our civil rights. In a recent study, 52 percent of those who knew gays personally favored ensuring our civil rights while only 27 percent of those who thought they did not know anyone gay favored the idea.

The Heterosexual Assumption—Correcting the Record

Another nonconfrontational way to combat bigotry is to simply correct the record when a nongay person assumes that you and your lover, or companions, are heterosexual. Since I am sixteen years older than my lover, we are exposed to the heterosexual assumption frequently in certain settings, nearly always those in which clothing is sold.

"Come over here and show your mom how you look in this jacket."

"Do you want to share the dressing room with your daughter?"

Or, true story, at Bloomingdale's, Terry gives me a hug and the salesperson says, "How nice to give your mom a hug."

Terry says, gently, "This is not my mother. She's my lover." The salesperson blanches. "Oh, I'm sorry. I just meant it's so nice to have a hug." Whereupon Terry gave *her* a hug, which she seemed to like quite a lot, or maybe she was just relieved to be forgiven for her politically incorrect gaffe.

The problem is that many heterosexuals don't have a context for two people of the same sex having intimate knowledge of each other unless they are related by blood—dad and son, mom and daughter (if there is an age difference); sisters, brothers, even cousins, if approximately the same age. When the context they perceive collapses, they are at a loss.

One night my lover and I and two gay male friends went to a wine-tasting dinner at a rather exclusive club. We were seated at a table with two older heterosexual couples who looked as if they rarely left Pasadena. Because we and our friends happened to sit male-female-male-female, the assumption was made that *we* were two straight couples. At some point the table conversation got around to who we all were and the question was asked jovially, "So how long are you folks married?" the questioner looking from one opposite-sex pair to the other. Our friend Dick said quietly, "We're not married. We're all gay."

"You're all paid?" the questioner repeated, somewhat alarmed.

Dick leaned forward and enunciated carefully, "No, I said we're all *gay*."

The questioner stared blankly at Dick. The context in which he had perceived us had collapsed and he didn't know where to go next. Dick smiled. We all smiled. They smiled. And, the conversation moved on to the Beaujolais.

While this was no great lesson in gay awareness, it was another instance in which the heterosexual assumption was not allowed to be made. We established the reality of who we were and the message that we *wanted* to be known as gay and lesbian people. That message, even so benignly delivered, can go a long way toward eroding the fixed notion that gay people have something to hide and to be apologetic about.

We are doing nothing to correct the record when we talk about ourselves in public and lower our voice when we say the word "gay." Heaven forbid others should know that gay and lesbian people are among them. But the heterosexual assumption is reinforced when we give no sign that we are anything but that. I know this is essentially habit when I hear people who are gay or lesbian *activists* lowering their voice.

The funniest experience I've had with this was when we were having dinner in a restaurant with the straight sister of an openly gay male friend. She was telling me about something and when she came to the word "heterosexual" she lowered her voice. I believe she was trying so hard to be politically correct she got mixed up. I reminded her that being heterosexual was nothing to be ashamed of.

A friend told me of the following incident which he happened to observe in a restaurant. Two gay men were having dinner. One was telling the other about a date he'd had with another man, going into some detail. Two straight men at the next table overheard this conversation and one then said loudly to the other, "Hey, you want some fruit salad?" And the other replied, mockingly, "Oh no, I can't eat a thing. My wrist is just too limp!"

One of the gay men rose, walked over to the straights, and placed his hands flat on the table. He was tall and broad shouldered and muscled. He said calmly, "Do you have a problem with me, because if you have a problem with me we can go outside and talk about it."

"No harm meant, no harm meant," the straight man said, nervously eyeing the physique of the man towering over him.

So much for correcting the record on limp wrists. Obviously this is not a tack for most of us to take, but any time we *don't* sit still for derogatory stereotyping we are challenging homophobia with the truth, and that is always a point in our favor.

Families in the Trenches

The movement for gay civil rights has a secret weapon. It is the accepting families of gay and lesbian people who have become activists on behalf of their children. They are the surprise that greets the legislators they lobby, the homophobes they confront in the media, the friends and families they educate about what it means to be gay or lesbian. They are strong and effective advocates in the fight against bigotry.

Formed in 1973, P-FLAG (Parents, Families and Friends of

Lesbians and Gays) has grown to be one of the four largest gay advocacy groups in the United States. They have local chapters in fifteen regions of the country. They conduct seminars and workshops on lesbian and gay issues all over the United States and publish informational materials designed to educate parents, and help their children come out to them.

The P. LAG members march and they protest, they build coalitions. They are visible models for other families struggling to understand and accept their gay sons and lesbian daughters. Their presence at any gay function—fund-raiser, parade, rally—is always met with wild enthusiasm for they stand in loco parentis to many gays and lesbians whose own families have not yet made it past their own prejudices.

P-FLAG is about organized advocacy, but there are also instances of individual families taking a stand to fight anti-gay bigotry. Take the Henigans of Fountain Valley in Orange County, California. Their story was told in the *Los Angeles Times* (February 9, 1994). It all began when some students at Fountain Valley High School wanted to start a gay and lesbian support group on campus. Mike Henigan was the school's athletic director and mom Adrienne was the college career specialist.

The Henigans had recently learned that their own gay son, Patrick, then in college, had suffered in silence during his high school days, repeatedly contemplating suicide. Mike and Adrienne had gone through the usual turmoil accepting their football hero son's gayness, but Mike was later quoted as saying, "How could I suddenly not love him for one part of his life being different than mine?"

About a month after the first meeting of the (gay and lesbian) Fountain Valley High School Student Alliance a group of students calling themselves the Future Good Boys of America launched an antigay campaign against the Alliance. As the homophobic protests grew more antagonistic with flyers and pickets, the Henigans began speaking at school board meetings, pleading for tolerance and support of the Alliance. They talked about Patrick's experience and that of the gay and lesbian students to whom they had given their individual support.

At a tense, crowded meeting of the district school board the Henigans read a letter from their son describing the misery he'd gone through as a high school student, the alienation, the thoughts of suicide.

The meeting was so volatile the police were called in to control the crowd. The gutsy Henigans carried the day. The Alliance won its right to meet on campus. The Future Good Boys of America disbanded. Mom Adrienne said, "We felt we weren't able to help Patrick, but if we could help one other kid who's going through the same lonely journey, we should. Even if it was one kid, we wanted them to know they weren't hated."

This ordinary family—dad a coach, mom a school counselor—had gone to bat for the gay and lesbian students of Fountain Valley High simply because they wanted to. They did it on their own, overcoming their natural reticence, going public, working to educate the other parents of this conservative Orange County school district.

With the four children the Henigans raised on a suburban cul-de-sac, they were likened by the *Times* to a "1950s television clan," which is supposed to make their progay activism all the more amazing. Of course, the *Times* didn't understand that it is families just like the Henigans who are truly our secret weapon in the fight against bigotry. They did what they did because it was the right thing to do, which is the motivation behind all authentic activism.

Throughout this book the emphasis is on how to manage direct encounters with homophobia. But there are many other ways for gay and lesbian people to fight bigotry—ways that involve how you live your life, how you talk about who you are, and what you choose to involve yourself in.

Actually, you are fighting bigotry every time you write a letter praising or criticizing a politician, send a check to a gay or gay-friendly candidate, organize a gay awareness program in your company, church, or school. You deal a blow to discrimination by correcting the record when the heterosexual assumption is made about you, without necessarily making it into a confrontation.

We are joined in our advocacy by important allies—families of gay people who work through the organization P-FLAG to reduce discrimination and enlighten society about what it means to be gay or lesbian. And our cause is strengthened by the actions of ordinary people, like the Henigans of California, a family who stepped forward to counter an antigay campaign in their son's high school because they thought it was the right thing to do.

When superstar Elton John talks casually about being gay in a television interview, singer Melissa Etheridge invites *People* magazine to visit her home and meet her female lover, acclaimed British actor and openly gay man Ian McKellen is knighted by Queen Elizabeth, and tennis great Martina Navratilova proudly identifies herself as a lesbian, new facets of the gay image must enter the consciousness of many nongay people. This is fighting bigotry with affirmation.

3

Understanding and Managing
Your Anger

I sat at lunch with several friends talking about different ways to respond in encounters with homophobes. One said that he thought that the most efficient way to deal with such a person would be to let the person know how you feel about what he or she said without being confrontive enough to stir things up.

I generously shared that I thought the trouble with him was that he was just not an angry person. My friend looked as if he weren't sure if this was a criticism or a compliment, but he agreed with me.

I went on to say that there are a lot of people out there who *are* angry and their anger is very close to the surface. It can be tapped into anytime, no deliberating on the most appropriate response—provocation triggers aggression. For an angry gay or lesbian person who has lived with prejudice and discrimination for years, homophobic provocation is likely to produce either an angry assault or flight to avoid being assaultive.

My friends wanted to know how angry people could be

helped to do something other than just striking out or fleeing when they are provoked.

I offered that three things are necessary: knowing what your triggers are, being able to monitor the arousal of anger, and learning to exercise self-control.

My first friend was skeptical, saying that he had known angry people who were always ready for a fight, and when challenged about this would say they couldn't help themselves. I countered that accepting that statement was just reinforcing their cop-out, that we all have more options in life than we are normally aware of.

If you challenge an angry person to behave in a nonaggressive way you have begun the process of breaking into a pattern of automatic acting out. That means that the person may feel anger but it does not always have to be expressed by angry *behavior*. It isn't what you feel, it's what you do about it.

In answer to a question about acting out one's anger I suggested that channeled anger can be very effective. Every social movement is born of anger over injustice, but those that are the most effective are the ones in which people channel their anger into forceful protest with a clear agenda for change.

To channel anger one must be aware of the storm signals—the distant early-warning signs of volatility. That awareness can cue the mechanisms of control. For instance, how we *label* the provocative act and what intent we attribute to the person doing the provoking is all important.

If the message you flash to yourself is: "Danger! The enemy! Attack!" there is no room for consideration of alternative responses. But if you catch yourself and *relabel* the situation, the message you send yourself might be: "Opportunity! Confused person! Seize the agenda! Expose! Educate!" Redefining the situation in this way is a mechanism of control.

My friends seemed intrigued by the idea of *strategies* for managing the anger that rises in us when we are faced with antigay bigotry. By circumventing the pattern of anger arousal leading to anger acted out, more choices become available for dealing with homophobia in whatever guise it is encountered. With control come the prerogatives of power.

Inspired by this conversation, I began to think about what it means to be angry, not the physiological but the psychological experience. Why do we get angry? What purpose does it serve? One prevailing theory is that anger is a defense against fear, a way of gaining a sense of personal control when vulnerability is felt. Becoming angry externalizes the experience so you can focus on an outside someone or something rather than having to deal with the internal stress that fear and vulnerability produce.

When we are under attack we feel vulnerable. A way to combat that vulnerability is to get mad. In this way anger has an adaptive function. It allows a transformation of energy from our fragile inner world to the more malleable outer world, over which we can exercise some influence. It feels better to be an angry person than a sacred and vulnerable person.

Anger also has a potentiating effect, enabling action over the tendency one might have in a given situation to be overwhelmed and passive. If you care about how others see you, anger can be adaptive in masking anxious and apprehensive feelings. The angry person is typically *seen* as more powerful than one who is expressing fear and anxiety. Anger also can serve to keep people at a distance, if that is a need you have. No one wants to grapple with a porcupine, even if it is a porcupine longing to be loved.

The problem is that anger can also be maladaptive if it leads to behavior that is destructive or to flight from the scene because feelings are out of control. The person who angrily acts out before thinking relinquishes the chance to use the provocation to educate, to change an intolerable situation, or to bridge the gap with another. Being angry can make one *feel* more potent, but managed anger bestows the ability to accomplish a purpose—to transcend powerlessness and act effectively.

Managing Anger

We have all demonstrated to ourselves that we can manage anger. If the telephone rings in the middle of a bitter fight with someone, we quickly shift our behavior to being polite and cordial. We "hold our temper" when the stakes are too high to express the hostility we feel—toward a caustic boss, an unreasonable and demanding customer, the attorney browbeating us in a cross-examination, a merciless traffic cop. We are managing our anger. We do it all the time.

I would never tell a gay or lesbian person *not* to be angry about the affronts we experience directly and indirectly in our lives. Anger is a healthy reaction to antigay bigotry, but when it erupts into out-of-control behavior it can render you ineffective.

Conversely, if your anger is so overwhelming that it immobilizes you at the very moment you want to be articulate and forceful, it is maladaptive—you have handed the other person an undeserved victory.

You want your anger to work *for* you. That means that you may be full of fury, but how you express that feeling is under your control. You have learned to get on top of the anger and use it to energize your reactions, but the nature and content of your responses are determined by what *you* want to accomplish, not by emotions out of control.

Channeled anger can be the fuel that you need to move ahead with an action that poses you as an adversary. Allowing your anger can be the best antidote to the fear that may accompany the anticipation of confrontation. The writer Paul Monette, as gentle a human being as there ever was, channeled his anger about AIDS through the pages of book after book, effecting a fierce condemnation of the forces he believed were impediments to finding a cure.

Paul's writing was energized by a willingness to let anger inform his vision of the struggle we must all go through to be agents of change in our own lives. By channeling his anger in the way he did he gave thousands of his readers permission to

feel their own anger as empowerment. He certainly did that
for me.

In the winter of 1993 I spent three weeks promoting a book
on radio talk shows and being gay-bashed. This experience
made me so angry I felt almost out of control. Striking back at
my attackers would have accomplished little, but I needed to
do something, so I wrote down everything they said—every
question, every comment. I thought through the best answers,
refined and refined them, organized and compiled them.

I ended up using my brain to create a reasonable way to
deal with unreasonable hostility. I channeled my own anger into
useful action, and one product of that action is this book. Had I
just stopped with the anger I think I would have a lingering bit-
terness that might inhibit any further attempts at trying to deal
with bigotry. Instead, I felt energized to continue to work on
the problem.

Of course, everyone isn't into writing books, but articulat-
ing your feelings about homophobic contacts, even if it's only
to a friend, is a way to put the experience in perspective, to externalize the anger and possibly formulate a tactic for dealing
with any such future experiences.

Do we always have the ability to channel anger? Not always,
for most of us. Have you been confronted with homophobic
comments that you desperately wanted to respond to, but the
rage building up in you caused you to be speechless?

Or have you ever just wanted to punch out the person who
is raucously telling a fag joke or carrying on about queers being
disgusting? If so, you are like me and like most of the gay and
lesbian people I've ever known. Being able to manage your
anger so that you can respond effectively gives you leverage you
can't have by simply exploding at the person provoking you, or
by being too immobilized to react at all.

In an effort to develop strategies for anger management in
homophobic encounters, I have put together some guidelines
for how to approach, cope with, and succeed in translating
anger into constructive action. These guidelines are based on

the work of various researchers in the fields of anger and stress management.* I propose four steps:

1) Anticipating and preparing for provocation.
2) Self-monitoring anger arousal.
3) Coping with the provocative event.
4) Self-reward.

1. Anticipating and Preparing for Provocation

Once you anticipate a homophobic encounter you can begin to prepare for it:

First, you should define for yourself what you are out to accomplish in this particular situation. Do you want to educate, facilitate a better relationship, or just get someone's homophobia out in the open? For instance:

"I want my parents to hear me out and understand what being gay means to me."

"I want this homophobe I'm on the TV program with to be seen for the bigot that he is."

"I want to convince management that they owe it to their loyal gay and lesbian employees to change their antigay policies."

Second, you should explore what you expect to happen. If you find you are having negative expectations, confront them. It would not be unusual if your pre-encounter messages to yourself were anything like these:

"I won't be heard."

"I won't be taken seriously."

"I'll get rattled and not be able to continue."

"I'll be humiliated."

"I'll be so mad I'll do something foolish."

"I'll get cold feet."

---

*Raymond W. Novaco, *Anger Control* (Lexington, Mass: D. C. Heath, 1975), and "The Functions and Regulation of the Arousal of Anger," *American Journal of Psychiatry* 133:10 (October 1976), pp. 1124–1127.

Only when such thoughts are out in the open can you deal effectively with them by reminding yourself of your positive intentions and by *planning* to be in charge of the encounter:

"It's the right thing to do."

"I'm doing this because I owe it to myself."

"I believe in my ability to do this."

"I will not back off."

"I will insist on being heard."

"I will not allow anyone to make a victim of me."

"I can control my anger."

Remember, you are already ahead of the game when you actually engage in the encounter. You are affirming yourself and breaking the conspiracy of silence that still too often thwarts dialogue between gay and nongay people.

Eddie could feel himself tensing up as he walked the few blocks from his apartment to the church. He knew what he was doing was right, but the prospect of confronting Mr. Ryerson made him nervous. Eddie was a gay father whose son, Timmy, had told him last night that his Boy Scout leader, Mr. Ryerson, said bad things about gay people in front of the whole troop. Timmy had felt angry at Mr. Ryerson but was too embarrassed to say anything.

Since Eddie was a single father, he'd always met Mr. Ryerson alone and didn't feel the need to say that he was gay, but when Timmy told him, with tears in his eyes, what Mr. Ryerson said, Eddie knew he had to take action.

Mr. Ryerson had said, "Homosexuals are people you don't want to get close to. They will try to make you believe they care about you but they can do you harm, so stay away from people like this."

Eddie shuddered at the thought of Timmy, or any of the other children, hearing so ridiculously menacing a warning. It was outrageous for Mr. Ryerson to be condemning people he obviously knows nothing about. Eddie was getting more and more riled as he thought about how this must have made Timmy feel. He told himself:

"I'd like to throttle this guy."

"What an irresponsible thing to do."

"Doesn't he know there might be boys with gay parents in his troop?"

"He must be some bigot, probably so entrenched he won't hear a thing I say."

Eddie was really furious now:

"I'll just have to punch him out, and make a real damn fool of myself."

"The more I think about it the madder I get."

"This bastard isn't going to care what I say."

"He's got his mind made up."

"I'll be batting my head against the wall."

Inundated by these negative messages, Eddie was headed for disaster, talking himself into feeling hopeless and helpless. If Eddie had had the benefit of learning the strategies of anger management, he would have been *preparing* himself in a different way. His messages to himself might have been more like the following:

"I'm going to confront a person whose bigotry is a dangerous force in my son's life."

"I owe it to myself and Timmy to do this."

"I'll insist that he hear me out."

"I can control my anger."

"I have something important to say and I won't back off. I can do this."

Now, by the time Eddie got to the church and into Mr. Ryerson's presence, he would have been more than ready for the encounter. His last-minute preparation for a successful experience would have primed him to move quickly and confidently into the confrontation.

Such self-instructional preparatory statements as Eddie might have used are an important part of most training programs on anger management. For instance, a study was done of people who work as abortion clinic escorts, suffering the insults, vicious name-calling, and sometimes physical assaults that antiabortion fanatics confront them with.*

Managing their anger and not retaliating in kind is a major challenge for these escorts. One woman escort would go home at night, stand in front of the mirror, and "scream back" at the protesters, until her family became alarmed. Another escort saw two men in a mall parking lot who were dressed in white shirts and ties similar to those worn by the fundamentalist extremists who blocked the clinic's doors. She had to fight an impulse to run them over with her car.

In their anger-management training it was especially important for these escorts to define their anger as "rational and morally appropriate" since they were protecting the legal right of women to make a choice about their own bodies. In preparing for their sometimes brutal encounters with the antiabortionists, they rehearsed responses they believed would preserve their perspective—they had a job to do, get these women safely inside the clinic door, period.

In the face of insults and assaults they told themselves:

"We're not crazy, they are."

"We're not immoral, they are."

To take the edge off their anger they shared humorous *fantasies* of retaliating against the protesters, enjoying a sense of personal control in fantasy that released them somewhat from the fear and resentment they lived with in reality. Preparing for provocation and debriefing their experiences afterward helped these courageous people withstand the hostility and aggression they encountered without responding violently and thereby discrediting their mission.

Given that abortion clinic escorts experience vilification

---

* Judith Diiorio and Michael R. Nusbaumer, "Securing Our Sanity: Anger Management among Abortion Escorts," *Journal of Contemporary Ethnography* 21, no. 4 (January 1993): xx–xx, pp. 411–438.

that has nothing to do with who they are as people, there seems a similarity to the experience of gays and lesbians, discriminated against, too often attacked, for reasons that have nothing to do with who we are as human beings.

While anticipation and preparation support constructive action in anger-producing situations, paradoxically, they can occasionally do just the opposite. We sometimes have a tendency to prepare ourselves for provocation based only on the similarity of a situation to one in which we *did* have a bad experience. The messages we give ourselves are just the *opposite* of the positive self-statements above:

"I'm not going to like this."

"They're going to give me a hard time."

"I don't know if I can handle my anger."

"I hate bigots."

"I'm angry already."

If you have doubts about the effectiveness of positive self-messages, you will easily see how common and how affecting negative messages to yourself can be. By the time you get where you're going, you have created a provocation within yourself. You don't even need the homophobic other. You have already *made yourself* angry.

Haven't we all done this at one time or another? I sometimes have to shut off the running dialogue in my head about how much I dislike this person, resent her, and distrust her in order to be able to interact with her in real time. She may or may not have done anything to deserve my antagonism, but I am so pissed off by my own thoughts that her culpability no longer even matters. *I* have provoked myself into an angry state.

If you find yourself doing this, one strategy is to substitute self-affirming messages for the provocative ones. That way you can release yourself from the angry feelings you have stirred up in yourself, the feelings that may inhibit your ability to function rationally in an encounter.

"I am competent to deal with this person no matter what she does."

"I'm a rational person, I can focus on my objective and put these angry feelings aside."

At the very least you will have given yourself a chance to deal with the *reality*, whatever it is, once you get there.

I appreciate how simplistic "talking to yourself" in these positive ways may seem, but words are affecting and most of us *do* talk to ourselves a lot. What I am really getting at is giving yourself a choice at a time when it may feel as if there are no choices. You're mad as hell and that's it. But that's not all there is to it. You can allow yourself the choice of managing your anger in order to have a constructive, satisfying experience. That can happen in the way you *prepare* yourself to meet a difficult situation.

2. Self-Monitoring Anger Arousal

You are in the encounter. You are aware that something different is happening inside you. You feel less in control than you did moments ago. The other person is being intransigent and infuriating. You are trying to marshal your strength to respond, but your thinking is constrained, unclear. You feel vulnerable, then angry, so angry you just want to strike out—do harm— punish. You feel an immobilizing tension in yourself.

Now it is time to talk to yourself again: "Okay, I am angry but I am also in control of myself. I will not personalize this, no matter what is said. Slow down. Respond calmly. Focus."

Marylou could hardly believe her eyes as she read over the termination report. "Violation of company policy on homosexuals." What did this mean? What policy? She'd worked at Stein-N-Burger for two years. She'd been led to believe she was a model employee. Her last evaluation was excellent. She'd had a raise. What happened? She never hid the fact that she was a lesbian. She just didn't talk about it, unless asked.

The new assistant manager had heard her talking on the

telephone to her girlfriend. He put two and two together and came up with the question:

"Marylou, are you homosexual?"

"I am a lesbian, yes. It's not a secret."

The next day she was fired.

Marylou decided that she needed to talk to the boss. She told herself that she would remain calm, that she would not be thrown by this. She just wanted an explanation and she wanted it right away. She marched into the front office and stood before the owner's desk.

"I'd like to know what this is all about. I've been a good employee for two years. Why are you suddenly firing me?"

The owner looked annoyed. "Marylou, we don't have homosexuals working here. It's company policy. We are a family-centered establishment and your kind don't reflect family values."

Marylou felt the anger rising in her.

"What are you talking about? Like I'm supposed to be some kind of menace to families? That's ridiculous!"

The owner answered in a patronizing voice, "Marylou, your kind is just not good for our business."

Marylou's mind suddenly went blank, as if this were too much for her brain to compute. All she could feel was a terrible helplessness, then anger, more anger than she had ever felt. She was speechless. All she could think about was how she'd like to smash in this man's face. While she stood mute and shaking before the owner, he returned to his paperwork.

Marylou felt rooted to the spot. She realized that her anger had taken over. She took a deep breath and began an internal dialogue.

"I'm not going to let my anger stop me. Hold on. Slow it down. Calm down. This may be my only chance to say what I have to say."

Marylou placed her hands on the owner's desk and leaned forward.

"I want to tell you how this makes me feel—betrayed, angry, and righteous because I know that I'm a good person and you know it too. You're a hypocrite. It's *your* kind that mocks love and loyalty. It's your kind that should be fired for immorality! I'm not finished with this!"

Marylou left the owner's office still very angry, but satisfied with herself. She knew she had been right and had been heard.

The arousal signals—anger building—are the cue to move on to the next step in the process of transforming anger into constructive action. This is the *opposite* of reacting automatically. Impulse is controlled. You are now ready to do the main work of anger management—reinterpreting the provoking event. You are giving your own meaning to the situation and acting out of your own needs, rather than reacting to someone else's agenda.

3. Coping with the Provocative Event

It's called "cognitive restructuring." It means simply that you modify the way you see a situation. Initially, you may see only that you have been affronted—insulted, stigmatized, trivialized. You take it in and feel it personally. You are hurt and angry. Then you begin to redefine what is happening.

This is not about you. It is about what this bigoted, uncomprehending person *wants* you to feel, or it is about his inability to deal with something new, or it is about his obsession with homosexuality. It's about him, not about you.

When you can move on from being personally affronted, you have a chance to examine what is really going on. You can gain perspective and proceed to the task at hand, whatever you have determined that to be—set the record straight, label anti-gay behavior for what it is, or challenge someone's well-meaning but distorted ideas about who you are. You are not preoccupied with anger. You are focused on the task. You have given yourself these messages:

"I will not take this personally."

"I can see what this person is doing."

"I know what I have to do."

"I will not be provoked into an attack."
"I will stick to what I am here to accomplish."

Gina felt annoyed at having to fill out the long questionnaire, but this was a new doctor for her and she realized the information was needed. When she came to the item called
"marital status," she felt more than annoyed. She stared at it
for a minute, then decided to leave it blank. Sometimes she
would put "not applicable," or "domestic partnered," but this
time she wrote nothing.

When Gina completed the form she handed it to the receptionist. A few minutes later the receptionist said, "Excuse
me, but you didn't finish this one item. Doctor likes to have
everything filled out. What is your husband's name?"

Gina wanted to swear at the young woman, but she said
awkwardly, "I do not have a husband." She was immediately
sorry she'd said it that way.

"Oh, so you're unmarried."

"No, I am very much married. I just don't have a husband."

Gina watched the young woman write, "unmarried."

"And this person to be notified in case of emergency. What
is her relationship to you?"

"She is my spouse."

Gina watched as the receptionist wrote, "friend." Something opened up in Gina then, a familiar feeling like running in
a dream and not getting anywhere. She felt rage at the blind-
ness of ignorant people, so free to trivialize your life. She
wanted to punish this person for the insult of being diminished, not being heard or understood. And then Gina suddenly
saw that her *reaction* was about being personally affronted but
the *situation* was about someone else's inability to deal with an
unfamiliar reality.

This redefinition freed Gina to externalize her focus, to see
that it was the questionnaire that was flawed, not her. The form
was a product of a behind-the-times medical office, or maybe it
was ignorance or laziness, or even a prejudiced point of view.

But it was not there to insult or humiliate her. Getting her anger under control allowed her to take another tack with the receptionist. She asked for a new copy of the form.

She pointed out to the bewildered young woman that the designations regarding marital status were too limited, that there were many people in the world, in their own community, who were gay or lesbian and in committed relationships that are like marriages in every way. Gina said that the form should reflect this.

She suggested that receptionists in medical offices would do well to recognize that gay and lesbian people do become patients and she, the receptionist, wouldn't want them all to be as angry with her as this patient was at this moment.

"Now, I'll just take this up with the doctor," Gina smiled.

The speechless young woman looked relieved.

4. Self-Reward

Since the objective of anger management is the development of a sense of personal competence in provocative situations, it is important that you reward yourself when you have any success at all, even moderate.

"I made it work."

"That wasn't as hard as I thought it would be."

"I'm getting better at this."

"I can control my anger."

"I can handle this kind of situation."

These self-messages serve to reinforce the belief in your ability to deal with provocation constructively. You are telling yourself that you can manage your anger effectively and you can exercise personal control no matter what the provocation is.

Your Anger Versus Theirs

It is important to note that your anger is of a different nature than that of the homophobic person provoking you. Their difficulty with you as a gay or lesbian person is not triggered by anything you've done to them. You are a symbol of something unfamiliar—a threat. They have defined you in the abstract as someone to fear and condemn.

Their hostility is all tangled up with their misinformation about what homosexuality is or, if it's okay, what it might do to them. Their personal agenda is to find a way to feel better about themselves and you are the vehicle for their doing that.

Your anger, on the other hand, is the result of something they *have* said or done to you or to others who are gay. You didn't provoke them except by your existence. Your anger is rational, theirs isn't, and that should put you at a distinct advantage in any encounter with them.

Anger and Internalized Homophobia

There is one subtle aspect of managing anger—particularly the kind that immobilizes you—that must be mentioned. If we have any conflicted feelings about being gay or lesbian, no matter how subtle, an antigay slur can pierce the outer layers of self-acceptance and shoot straight inside to that soft place where our own self-doubts keep us vulnerable.

These conflicting feelings about being gay may not even be entirely conscious, but they can be immobilizing nevertheless. The condemnation from another, spoken or implied, taps into the condemnation of self that has been there all along. Provocation renders one defenseless when it echoes the same repudiation that is going on inside. How important it is, therefore, to root out that conflict, see it for what it is, and do the work of self-affirmation.

It's hard for me to believe that we don't all have that vulnerable place in us—the consequence of growing up in a homophobic society and living with antigay prejudice in our everyday lives. But we can defend against its ability to immobilize us when we are provoked. The key is to stay focused on the external trigger—someone else's need to judge, to reject, to punish, to wound.

There is much to be angry about if you are a gay or lesbian person. Making your anger work for you requires discipline and a willingness to forgo the gratification of dealing with antigay prejudice by violent physical or verbal assault, or by flight. The ideal is to feel the anger, even the rage, but know how to talk yourself into a mode of thinking that keeps you in touch with what you are there to accomplish. You are present, focused, and in charge of the action.

4

Why People Hate—The Origins of Prejudice

The Prevalence of Hatred

Everyone is a potential hater.

Aggression is a part of every person's makeup. Depending on one's family training, the culture one lives in, and the circumstances of one's life, aggression is expressed openly, covertly, or repressively. Various social mechanisms do provide acceptable outlets for aggression. One such outlet is declared warfare, in which wounding or killing other people is not only excused but celebrated and rewarded.

Another outlet is organized sports. You need only observe a well-attended athletic event to experience the intensity of feeling generated by the *sanctioned* expression of hostility during competition. One affiliates with a particular team and the other team is the "enemy." It is okay to act out belligerently toward the enemy by shouting scornfully at the opposing players during competitive play.

This is an acceptable vehicle for the aggression that might

otherwise be acted out in a way that would bring harm to an innocent victim. In that regard organized sport provides an important service to the society; it contains aggression and makes the world a slightly safer place to be.

One need only think about the implications of this to get a hint of the potential for hatred that exists just below the surface of many human transactions. To understand the influence of this emotion on personal behavior, we must look at its role in the psychological life of the individual, any individual, even you or me.

Why Do People Hate?

Sometimes people hate because they are unable to love. Actually, love and hate have a lot in common. They both excite, stir passion, come from deep within, and remind you that you are alive. You have probably been in love and can remember the rush of emotion you experienced when the object of your affection walked into a room.

But there are those for whom love is anything but a welcome visitor, for whom it is a dangerous emotion that makes you vulnerable and defenseless. Love carries with it the potential of oppressive responsibility. You are expected to have relationships with the people you love, to care about their well-being, to selflessly support and protect them.

Hate, on the other hand, makes no such demands. You don't have to form relationships with people you hate. You don't have to care about what is happening to them. You don't even have to relate to them as human beings. Hating others creates an illusion of superiority and strength, which works as protection against those who are different enough to be threatening.

Hating helps to make the world seem more manageable by reducing many of the complexities of life to simple concepts: good and evil, right and wrong, safe and dangerous. These concepts are not seen as oversimplified abstractions. They are the true guideposts of the hater's journey through life, defined by one "authority" or another, ways to know that you are okay because someone else isn't.

Hating can provide those who are powerless with "explanations" for what is wrong in their world. *"They"* are ruining everything. Pat Robertson says, in a public speech, that homosexuality is a "shameful lifestyle that destroys all it touches."

Even though this statement makes no sense at all, it provides the powerless person with a compelling reason to hate homosexuals, "who are ruining everything." That is a significant part of what hating strangers is about—a target to aggress against—toward whom anger can be discharged with little or no fear of retaliation.

Oddly enough, the passion of hatred is not too far removed from the passion of romantic love. It can be as preoccupying, and as co-opting of rational thought. Hatred can be as compelling and all-consuming as the lust of sexual desire. That is what makes it so frightening, the intensity that seems to make no sense in terms of the object of the hatred, the stranger.

It makes no sense because it isn't really about the hated person or group at all. It's about the hater's need to get lost in the feelings, the excitement, the perception of power over the victim. A victim is therefore as indispensable to the hater as the inamorata is to the romantic lover.

Like people who are in love with love, there are people who are in love with hate, probably for many of the same reasons: You feel stimulated, involved, worthwhile when you love. You feel the same way when you hate.

Hating often serves an important purpose for the self-esteem of the hater in that it is used to justify antipathy toward a person or group who can then be blamed for what is wrong in one's life, making it possible to abdicate responsibility for doing something about one's own failures and misdeeds.

Many of those who go for the *passion* of hatred—the skin-heads, rednecks, and street gangs—hate not only for the high of hating, but also to prove their competence and worth. Given the irrationality of their thinking and the primitive needs they are seeking to fulfill, they can only express themselves through mindless violence in some form. Unless one is prepared to meet violence with more violence, the best recourse is to get out of their way, to refuse to become the victim they need to prove how powerful they really are.

The homophobic haters who hide behind their piety or their patriotism are no less drawn by the passion of hating and the opportunity to establish their superiority, but they are more subtle and devious about it. The important task with them is to unmask their hypocrisy. They will rarely own up to hating homosexuals. They will more likely present themselves as defenders of the faith, or advocates of "traditional family values."

Who Hates?

No one is a born hater. The newborn revels in including, and being included by, everyone in its environment. Babies smile to show their delight with the people around them and strive to get back from those same people similar signs of approval. It is, in a sense, a love feast that sets the foundation for the child's ability to develop trust, a sense of security, and comfort with the expression of affection.

It is through these interactions that the child gets its affilia-tive needs met, an important part of the emotional develop-ment that prepares us for the relationships of our adult life. But what happens when baby's affiliative needs are not met, when frustration replaces contentment because the adult caretakers are negligent or unresponsive, or inconsistent in their expres-sions of approval—smiling in one encounter, harsh and irritated in the next?

The developing child feels insecure, threatened, and confused. The pain of vulnerability gives way to a self-protective rejection of emotional openness. The child grows up suspicious of the motives of others, defensively excluding people rather than including them, and intolerant of anything that might compromise a delicately balanced sense of equilibrium.

The stage is now set for the playing out of a life drama organized around two needs: 1) resisting change because the unknown is dangerous, and 2) identifying "enemies" on whom to displace unresolved anger for the pain caused by childhood neglect or abuse.

These are the people to whom loving with an open heart feels dangerous because they are already too hurt to allow another person access to the vulnerable inner self. They tend to have controlled relationships that do not demand too much intimacy. On the outside they look like good citizens who lead exemplary lives. On the inside they are embattled, always wary of someone getting past the barriers, too frightened of betrayal to allow love.

Their emotional highs come from the hatred they feel for individuals and groups whom they have demonized, usually in concert with others similar to them, often endorsed by religious "authority." These are the core constituents the demagogues recruit offering approval, affiliation, and protection—the very things that were missing in the early lives of these people.

So some people learn to hate because they have been cheated of nurturing love in their development. They come to substitute the emotional high of hating for the passion of loving. This is the psychopathology of bigotry.

This is how hatred takes root in the individual psyche and is then tapped into by the demagogues to build a political constituency founded on human vulnerability. These are the people you might personally encounter at some time in your life, or more likely, they are the people your loving old auntie might encounter and from whom she gets her prejudices reinforced.

Understanding Prejudice

I have described some of the attitudes and ideas that are used by people to justify their hatred. What I have described are their prejudices.

One dictionary definition of *prejudice* is:

> An adverse opinion or leaning formed without just grounds or before sufficient knowledge; an irrational attitude of hostility directed against an individual, a group, a race, or their supposed characteristics.

Since prejudice is defined as an attitude that is irrational, hostile, and without basis in fact, why would people hang on to such ideas? Of course, *they* don't identify their ideas as irrational, hostile, or unfounded. To the contrary, such ideas often form the cornerstone of an individual's, a family's, a community's belief system—that set of ideas and attitudes that influence the standards by which people conduct their lives.

Unless there is a reason to be analytical about one's belief system, and more often than not there isn't, the fact that prejudices are passed from generation to generation gives them an aura of authority and truth, even when they are products of folklore and fantasy with no grounding in reality.

You have, no doubt, been exposed to ideas in your own family that you later discovered to be more about superstition than fact. It is unlikely that you will pass on those ideas as gospel, but possibly fragments will get integrated into your thinking, since the hold that family custom has on us all can be very strong.

What compels individuals to stay invested in their prejudices? It's handy for one thing. It makes life easier to have beliefs that appear to define what's okay and what isn't about other people's behavior, and more importantly, about one's own behavior.

Prepackaged judgments about right and wrong feel safer

because they are shared with other like-minded people—there is the endorsement of majority thinking and a reason not to have to do the hard work of figuring out the morality of every situation life presents. The problem is that in this process stereotypes and the other hallmarks of bigotry are perpetuated and sanctioned by religious and political groups with self-serving agendas.

A major conduit of prejudice is the family. Where strong prejudices exist in a family their influence becomes part of the socialization of the children. Will these individuals retain their prejudices once they reach adulthood? Many of us grew up in prejudiced families.

The draw of attitudes originating in the formative years is very powerful. It is only when equally powerful ideas impact our belief system in adulthood that prejudices learned early will likely be moderated or relinquished. How close one stays to the family culture is the key.

In my experience, gay and lesbian people who have left the family fold to live their adult lives (that's most of us) have been able to move away from family prejudices as well. Having been exposed to unfounded antigay and lesbian bigotry, you probably have also learned to reject intolerance more quickly than your heterosexual counterparts.

This is not to say that we gay and lesbian people have no prejudices. One need only to look at the tensions between the greater gay and lesbian community and our minority brothers and sisters to know that prejudice is alive and well in our gay world. But I believe that in the main we are less likely to be co-opted by the prejudices we learned in our families because we tend to move away from the family culture more often, and more quickly, than nongay people tend to do.

One family culture that people have particular trouble moving away from is that based in the Mormon religion. Mormon families impose strict rules on how their adult children should live their lives. If these children as adults do not move away from the Mormon culture, the likelihood is that all learned prejudices will be kept intact along with everything else that is part of the Mormon family's teachings.

While the lessons of Mormonism are largely about healthy living, much of their teaching is highly prejudicial to anything that does not follow the Mormon religion. To ask these people to question their prejudices is to challenge the monolith of Mormon theology.

Even when a given family culture is not as binding as that of the Mormons, some adult children never grow independently of the family, never become truly self-defining individuals. Such people need to continue to please mom and dad, either directly, or as they have internalized them.

These folks spend the rest of their lives courting parental approval by not deviating from what they were taught as children. To ask these people to question their family's prejudices is to ask them to defy and rebel against their loved and feared parents.

A third condition that often insures adults will have the same prejudices as their families has to do with the way they were disciplined as children. If their parents were harsh disciplinarians, using authoritarian methods to teach obedience, it is likely the adult child will have an authoritarian personality— what social psychologists identify as the "prejudiced personality"—rigid thinking, intolerant, and punitive.

Another version of the prejudiced personality results when individuals are taught obedience by parents who threaten the withdrawal of love as a major means of discipline. The child's life is spent figuring out how to earn affection and avoid abandonment. These people grow up feeling insecure and fearful, angry at parents but unable to express that anger or, often, to even admit it to their own consciousness.

These are the candidates to become hard-core haters—full of unresolvable rage, ready to displace their hostility on any group. They hate Jews, blacks, "women libbers," fags, dykes, all foreigners, anyone different from them and identifiable as "dangerous." Their reservoir of anger is never depleted because they don't get to express it to the appropriate people—the parents who caused their anguish in the first place.

These are the kinds of people who are most likely to perpetuate an unbroken cycle of bigotry generation after generation. They replicate the culture they grew up in, usually complete with the kinds of discipline and the rules of love they experienced in their own families. Their prejudices are embedded in their view of the world, a view they pass on to their children. This is prejudice as *legacy*, unquestioned because to do so would be to confront fears too deep to fathom, or resentments too threatening to deal with.

While prejudice as legacy is the most common way people come by their intolerance, it is not the only way. Sometimes prejudice is more simply a product of what is happening in the person's contemporary life. The ability to deal with frustration is the key factor here, especially when the source of the frustration is too formidable or too undefinable to come to grips with.

We have all experienced situations in which we were frustrated about something happening, or not happening, but the source of the frustration was something so remote, or so large and powerful, that we didn't know how to get at it. For instance, a major agency of government fails to manage a part of the economy judiciously and we all suffer financially in our private lives. Whom do you blame—the Treasury Department, the Federal Reserve, the Office of Management and Budget? All are too remote and abstract to aggress against.

Instead, we blame the illegal immigrant who is "stealing our jobs, and costing us money in medical and social services." Conservative politicians identify illegal immigrants as a cause of our failing economy and people buy it because it's easier to be mad at a Mexican day laborer whom we can deprive or deport than at an amorphous government program that wasn't run right.

Or, to bring it closer to home, the frustration-aggression pattern is at work when you have had a terrible day at work but you can't get any satisfaction from yelling at clients or the boss, so you come home and find some minor transgression by your lover to yell at.

Presumably, anyone reading this book is too much of an animal lover to take it out on the dog, but it just might happen that your canine best friend is barking incessantly while you are trying to hear on the telephone and you are so frustrated you go overboard in your aggressive attempts to shut the little dear up.

Another example of the playing out of the frustration-aggression cycle occurs in the often tension-ridden situation of family relationships. For those who cannot manage the frustrations of their own family relationships, gay and lesbian people—"out to destroy the family"—make good targets on whom to displace aggression.

Since the prejudiced personality is someone who is rigid, suspicious, intolerant, and punitive, it is unlikely this person will be able to sustain nurturing, supportive, loving family relationships. Unable to identify or face this failure, the individual seeks someone to blame—to aggress against.

Ironically, these family failures are often the people one hears mouthing the rhetoric of the religious right regarding preservation of "family values." Typical of the prejudiced personality, their own family problems are not seen as a product of *their* actions but are the fault of a predatory outside force.

Unable to aggress against a deteriorating economy, politicians who lie and betray, crime that makes everyday life unsafe—all too formidable—beleaguered citizens seek to take out their frustration on any vulnerable minority—ethnic, racial, religious, or sexual:

"The Jews are conspiring to own the country."

"Reverse discrimination kills my opportunities because I'm white and the blacks get all the good scholarships and admissions to professional schools."

"Special interest groups, like gays, are dictating the political agenda."

"Third world refugees are draining us dry."

"The country is in moral decay because homosexuals are trying to convert everyone to their lifestyle."

Whether inherited or originating in one's contemporary life, prejudice is always irrational in that it generalizes from the few to the many, and is based on misinformation or distorting stereotypes in the first place. The fact that prejudice serves a psychological purpose for individuals makes it difficult to combat.

Logic, information, and rational debate do not make a dent when you are dealing with a person who is beset by fears about earning a living, functioning sexually, being an adequate spouse, being accepted and valued by others, or just staying sane in an unpredictable world.

The rationale for aggressing against homosexuals is the conviction that we are the predators who are undermining the American way of life. One problem is that "the American way of life" being lamented hasn't existed for quite some time now, but it is essential for the frustrated individual to hang on to the idea that something has gone terribly wrong and there is an identifiable villain around whom it's okay to hate.

Stereotyping—attaching derogatory labels—reduces complex human beings to one, or a few, traits which reinforce prejudices that in turn justify discrimination. Bigotry is about status and power, and stereotyping enables one group to maintain power over another group by controlling the way the victim group is seen by others. An example of this would be Senator Sam Nunn showing the American public how close the bunks are on board navy ships, illustrating the ease with which promiscuous gays, unable to control their sexual urges, could create havoc in the U.S. military.

Prejudice and discrimination are morally contemptible, but they are not immune to modification. Social psychologists teach us that while attitudes are hard to change, behavior is much easier. Racial integration affected the racist attitudes of many whites when they were forced to associate with blacks and learn that their negative stereotypes did not hold up.

Of relevance here is something called the *psychology of inevitability* that operates in situations of group conflict. When people are convinced that a change is going to take place—integration of the races, women in male-dominated careers—the tendency is to accept the inevitable.

For instance, when openly gay and lesbian people are integrated into the military, acceptance will eventually occur, as it has with African-Americans. The exceptions will be with those people whose prejudices are so rooted in religion, or their own shaky emotional adjustment, that accepting integration will seriously compromise their sense of well-being.

Most likely, the holdouts will have to remove themselves from the situation, or if they stay they will be dedicated gay-bashers. Then it will be up to the military leadership to decide what to do with the threat to cohesion and good order these recalcitrant homophobes represent.

While prejudice is often the result of profound forces at work in the society or in the individual's own life experience, there are times when the purpose it serves is much more elementary. For many people, familiarity equals security. They feel safe only when they are surrounded by people who look and behave like them. When the human landscape around them changes very much, they are threatened. They have to do something either to force the deviants out, or at least punish them for being who and where they are.

The problem is that the world has become so small, and the movement of people in it so uncontrolled, that trying to maintain homogeneity in one's personal environment is now close to impossible, especially in our larger cities. So, individuals threatened by diversity are left with either adjusting, or waging psychological (or physical) war on their unwanted neighbors.

For example, as we gays and lesbians are living more openly, nongay people may suddenly feel their neighborhoods are being overrun by homosexuals. We were there the whole time, of course, but they didn't notice. Now we are hiding who we are much less and there is in some quarters the perception that our numbers have alarmingly increased.

"We're here. We're queer. Get used to it!" But many people are not ready to "get used to it." They don't want foreigners everywhere they go (but they're there) and they don't want queers everywhere they look (but we're here). They don't want change at all (but it's happening). They are frustrated and they have to take it out on someone—the scapegoat.

5

Scapegoating: What It Is, How to Deal with It

In an ancient Hebrew ritual, on the Day of Atonement, a live goat was chosen by lot, the high priest laid both his hands on the goat's head and confessed over it the iniquities of the children of Israel. The sins of the people having thus been symbolically transferred to the beast, it was taken out into the wilderness and let go. The people felt purged and, for a while, guiltless.

These are the origins of the term *scapegoat* described here by Gordon Allport, the social psychologist whose work on prejudice and scapegoating is considered classic. It was primitive thinking that enabled the children of Israel to believe the goat could take the rap for their own "sins."

Just as the ancient Hebrews felt righteous once they had transferred their guilt to the goat, modern-day bigots feel morally redeemed once they rearrange reality so that the victim becomes the villain.

You, a gay or lesbian person, become the *victim* of someone's antigay prejudice, but the form that person's rhetoric takes presents you as the *villain* who is threatening the welfare of nice people going about their decent heterosexual lives. Whatever guilt bigotry embraces is transferred to the scapegoat. The bigot is redeemed and righteous.

The language of prejudice may be learned early, usually in the bosom of the family. It is honed in the streets and the school yards and subtly reinforced in many venues of religion. Scapegoating is a way to act out one's prejudices. The society obligingly tags minority groups each with its own mark of inferiority: Blacks are intellectually inferior, Hispanics are lazy, Asians are stealthy, and gays are sexual predators.

Promoting these negative stereotypes there is something for everyone to put down. The party line is that people who are "inferior" may pose a danger to us and must earn our disdain. We are justified in discriminating against them. They deserve what they get. Beating them up, name-calling, shutting them out of our neighborhoods, our workplaces, our lives is acceptable because they threaten our way of life.

This is the distorted process by which bigotry preserves its power. A necessary element in the process is the scapegoat, someone, some group to project evil onto to justify punishing them. Demeaning the scapegoat allows one to feel good about his/her own state of being, however flawed.

Another purpose served by scapegoating minorities is that of social control. Keep these people who are "different" intimidated enough and they will stay in their place, not disturb the status quo. People who are under attack find it difficult to mobilize their resources. Assimilation becomes a matter of survival and is inimical to *change*—what the bigot is trying mostly to prevent. For those who cannot assimilate, or blend in, intimidation is key to controlling their ability to challenge the dominant society.

Take for instance what we as gay and lesbian people are often enough told:

"Don't push yourselves on us."

"Don't call so much attention to yourself."
"Just be like everyone else."

In other words, just fade into the background and don't bother us. Above all don't try to change us. Gay and lesbian people are not cooperating with that these days and the bigots don't like it, so they have stepped up the level of intimidation in an effort to keep us under control.

What Motivates Scapegoating?

Gordon Allport, in his book *The Nature of Prejudice*, attributes the prejudice behind scapegoating to a combination of irrational hostility and erroneous generalizations—"thinking ill of others without sufficient warrant." Irrational hostility may be caused not only by personal failure but by the failure of larger systems—religion, the economy, education—to provide the tools and the wherewithal to thrive in a society growing more complex every day. Some people have an all-abiding anger at life. Any target will do if it promises relief from their tension.

The scapegoater has to feel he/she is always right. The goat is there, after all, to absorb whatever negative forces the scapegoater is needing to escape. No doubts, or recriminations, no compassion for the "victim," no new information, no questioning of beliefs. Prejudices are the rationale for the redeeming discriminatory act.

Who Are These Scapegoaters?

To give us a better understanding of the scapegoating process, Gordon Allport describes the conditions under which certain people feel justified in their hostile actions toward strangers who have never done anything to them. To know how to deal with scapegoaters in your own life, it is useful to make distinctions among them in terms of the personal needs their behavior might be serving. The following definitions are based on All-port's ideas about scapegoating.

1. The Compulsive Scapegoater

These are personally disordered individuals whose paranoid thinking necessitates an identified enemy to punish. They always feel under attack and are therefore always mobilized to counterattack. They are, in a sense, at war with themselves, but anger is turned outward because to turn it inward would make life impossible.

This person's anger is the product of a belief system that narrowly defines reality. Everyone is seen as dangerous. The threat is from the inside, a fragile, vulnerable inner self. For this person interpersonal connections don't usually happen. He/she is too isolated, too embattled to have loving relationships; instead, hatred is the emotion that is sustaining.

How to Deal with the Compulsive Scapegoater. It is usually wisest for you not to engage at all with this kind of individual. A gentle acknowledgment of the anger he or she is feeling is enough, maybe even too much, to do anything but stir up more hostility. There is no room for logic here. You cannot effectively address the demons inside a person who is unaware that his or her anger is generated by a fear of being destroyed.

The question is how do you know when you are faced with a compulsive scapegoater under the control of a pathological belief system? The clue, I think, is that the person *is* his or her anger. Whether it's racist, sexist, or homophobic, it doesn't matter. The anger shines through the content, and is unabating.

If this person trusts anyone at all it will be someone who shares the same embattled mind-set. Some skinheads are compulsive scapegoaters. It is their hatred that binds them together and must be kept going to justify that bond. They strike out against innocent victims in their fantasy war against imaginary enemies.

Doing battle with a compulsive scapegoater—skinhead or the angry person you might encounter anywhere in your life—is a no-win game. Better to leave their handling to law enforcement or the mental health establishment.

2. The Thwarted Scapegoater

This person has trouble coping with problems in a realistic and adaptive manner, and tends to handle frustration with aggression. The excitement of aggressing offsets the disappointments of a thwarted life. These individuals will demonstrate less irrationality than the compulsive types, and will be more responsive to your comments.

The payoff for the thwarted scapegoater is in the emotionality of the encounter. It is the engagement itself that is appealing because one can feel *potency* in creating conflict. If you can't bring order to your own life, you can bring disorder to someone else's.

This person probably was not taught good coping skills in his or her early life. Perhaps parents were too distracted, or overwhelmed, or didn't have those skills to teach. With no adequate ways to handle frustration, the thwarted scapegoater projects fault onto another and strikes out rather than looking inward for solutions.

How to Deal with the Thwarted Scapegoater. It is important to be able to understand that the anger you are dealing with here is not about who you are but about this person's own disappointments and feeling of impotence. Your challenge is to get *your* message across. Interrupting, talking over your excited opponent is fair play with this kind of individual because you are competing with the emotional rush that is driving the person's encounter with you.

I am reminded of a client, I'll call her Alice, who had been estranged from her family for some years because they could not deal with her being a lesbian. Happily ensconced in a loving relationship, Alice decided to try once more to heal the rift. She contacted her sister and talked about wanting to get together to talk.

Alice's sister immediately rebuffed her, saying angrily that my client's "lifestyle" was disgusting and how dare she even think of being part of a decent family. Alice was no longer willing to passively accept such nonsense and she began to argue with her sister. She pointed out that in this decent family their father had been abusive to all of them; their mother had suffered from debilitating bouts of depression as a result, and she, the sister, had been married and divorced three times.

These observations caused the sister to go into high gear about nothing being as dysfunctional as homosexuality, which was a perversion and a disgrace. When Alice tried to tell her sister that she just didn't understand, her sister began yelling that Alice was the bad seed in the family and hadn't she caused enough trouble already.

Alice, having worked through her own internalized homophobia in therapy, simply talked over her sister, saying that the trouble was caused by an unwillingness on the part of the family to try to understand their own prejudice, that it was time for all of them to look inside and deal with their own failings rather than scapegoating her.

In one of the rare moments that Alice's sister stopped to take a breath she seemed to hear this last message. Alice began to feel that there might be hope after all.

3. The Conventional Scapegoater

This person is thoroughly conventional and conservative, a churchgoer, though not deeply religious, and patriotic in the most shallow sense (flag waving and mouthing platitudes about God and country). The conventional scapegoater is a joiner who maintains security through identification with safe in-groups whose cohesion is sustained by putting down outsiders.

These people may be the most maddening—pious, righteous, trite, and condescending—avoiding responsibility for their own attitudes and acts by relying on assertions that "most people" feel as they do (find homosexuality abominable and abnormal, etc.). Feeling justified in their behavior because "it's what everybody believes," they will smugly tell you what's wrong with your gay or lesbian life.

The conventional scapegoater is usually someone who was brought up in an environment characterized by sameness—people looked and thought the same, life was contained and lived by the rules, those who deviated from the norm in any way were ostracized. The lessons learned were don't challenge the rules and don't stray outside the conventional guidelines.

I was told a story recently that disturbingly illustrates how the lessons that produce conventional scapegoaters are perpetuated.

A friend went to her nephew's eighth-grade graduation. The speaker was a local politician who told these twelve- and thirteen-year-olds that they should always remember that God would take care of them as long as they had a life that was about family and following tradition. He warned them that there were evil forces that might try to make them think differently from their family and their religion but they should resist these forces and hold on to what they had learned from the Bible and their own family as a way to live.

My friend was appalled since this event was taking place in a *public school*. The intimation was that we are all the same here and that's the way we want to keep it. In many places indoctrination into a philosophy of exclusion of differences and resistance to change occurs early. This becomes the philosophy of the conventional scapegoater, for whom gay and lesbian people can represent a threat to everything held dear.

How to Deal with the Conventional Scapegoater. Since the conventional scapegoater wears being part of the majority like a suit of armor, one task here is to pierce that armor by insisting on the truth, for instance that the person's homophobic statements are expressions of *individual prejudice for which he/she must take personal responsibility.*

It is important that each "most people feel this way" be challenged: "How do you know most people feel this way? Have you done a survey?" "Are you talking about your own friends and relatives and acquaintances?" "Where do you get the information about 'most people'?"

What you should try to focus on here is the Conventional Scapegoater's complacency about the rightness of actions that are assumed to be sanctioned by the majority. You can call the complacency into question by repeatedly going back to the individual's own *personal* attitudes and values. "But what do *you* think?" "What do *you* feel about this?"

It is likely that your own homophobic encounters may be with conventional scapegoaters, people in your family, workplace, or community who are not haters or out to do you in. They are good people who learned their prejudices early in life and have never had them seriously challenged. If you are a gay or lesbian person who is motivated to educate those you care about rather than writing them off, your first task is to *never* accept the rationale that prejudice is okay because "that's how everybody feels."

4. The Conforming Scapegoater

This is the true believer who has never really learned to think independently and relies on what the crowd is doing to know what to do. Little or no thought is given to the consequences of discriminatory acts. If everyone else is doing it, that's good enough. This person does not affiliate with groups to be safe and accepted, but simply "follows the crowd" mindlessly.

People who are conforming scapegoaters like having their time structured for them so they don't have to plan or make decisions. In the same way they like their opinions structured for them. The "erroneous generalizations" of Allport's definition of prejudice are easy to come by for these folks.

Stereotypical thinking compensates for the inability or the unwillingness to think analytically. Many people do not want to think at all. It is too much trouble or too demanding. They want to be fed fast-food ideas. They want to feel smart without having to learn anything. They are the blank pages on which institutionalized bigotry writes its destructive myths.

You know this person, the kind of apathetic individual who joins a crowd just to see what is happening. If the crowd is watching someone getting beaten up or murdered and is doing nothing, this person will do what everyone else is doing, nothing. If the crowd is harassing a gay or lesbian person this individual will join in the harassment even though he/she has no idea what has precipitated the attack.

This is essentially a bystander who attends events because they are there, like a perpetual movie extra who knows where to stand and what noises to make but hasn't a clue what the movie is really about. Are these people dangerous? Yes, because they are the unknowing pawns who allow themselves to be moved around the game board at will, implementing the plans of those who are opposed to gay and lesbian people even being in the game.

How to Deal with the Conforming Scapegoater. These individuals are probably the most easily derailed since attitudes and opinions are not rooted in their personal belief system. Since you are mainly competing with apathy here, your approach should be personal and motivational, not intellectual or combative.

For instance, you can offer your admiration and affection if the person will listen to your side and consider questioning the prejudices that have motivated his or her actions. Charm, humor, promises of some kind of reward are possibilities when dealing with someone whose apathy is the main thing holding him or her to a given opinion.

Let us say you are at a family reunion and you are seeing your distant cousins for the first time in years. You have shared with most of your family that you are gay but these folks haven't been clued in. They live in a small town and their lives are narrowly bound by the routines and customs of their unsophisticated community.

Someone in the family asks you about a gay activity you have been publicly involved in. The cousins, hearing this, look puzzled. They ask what that means. You talk about your project in a matter-of-fact way. One of the cousins interrupts to ask, incredulously, if you are a homosexual. You answer in the affirmative. The cousins display their disbelief. How could someone related to them be queer?

It so happens you are not surprised by the question and are ready to take this on. You ask them what the problem is with someone being gay? They act amazed and present all the negative stereotypes that are only too familiar. When you ask where they got these ideas you are told that *everyone* thinks this way. You point out the incorrectness of that. They look at you like you're crazy. Everyone they know thinks this way.

One by one you refute the negative stereotypes, cajoling the cousins to become more knowledgeable about one of the hottest issues of the day. When they do listen you reward them with a compliment about their interest in new ideas. When they seem even slightly convinced of something you say you reinforce them with an appreciation of how "open" they are.

By the end of the conversation the cousins are hooked, on you, if not your point of view. They like the way you treat them and in order to have the benefit of your company they hear a lot more about what it means to be gay and what it means to be blindly prejudiced about it.

The task is to somehow motivate the conforming scapegoater to move over to your side, where they will have your attention and admiration. They may not yet be sold on the correctness of your side but they are sold on you. The next step, of course, is to convince them that your side is the right side, the one that all the right people are part of.

5. The Calculating Scapegoater

This is the skillful demagogue who specializes in exploiting the fears and frustrations of the compulsive, thwarted, conventional, and conforming scapegoaters. This person knows how to organize around a "common enemy," to promise salvation, to build cohesion, and to stir up anger, all of which are used to build a constituency from which personal aggrandizement, money, and political power flow.

While the calculating scapegoater is satisfying her/his own needs, as is true for the other types of scapegoaters, there is a larger issue operating here. This individual is usually a spokesperson for an organized campaign to promote hatred and victimize targeted minority groups. Mobilized against gay and lesbian people is an array of organizations, most affiliated with the radical right element in fundamentalist Christianity.

In their war of moral terrorism against gays and lesbians, the weapon of choice for the calculating scapegoaters of the religious right is the Bible. While *old-time* fundamentalism is what they preach, their modus operandi is ultramodern sophisticated computerized direct-mail appeals. They exploit the fear of differentness and ignorance about homosexuality to recruit the constituents and money that translate into political clout.

These calculating scapegoaters are *political professionals*. Their agenda exploits gay and lesbian people because there is sufficient unquestioned prejudice already out there to build their case on. The accrual of power for them is in organizing their followers around antigay bigotry. The followers in turn reward them with money for the cause, votes in elections, and a grassroots work force to help spread the message of hate.

How to Deal with the Calculating Scapegoater. It is unlikely in the course of your daily life that you will personally encounter many calculating scapegoaters. Should you have the good fortune, however, to find yourself actually debating one of these professional homophobes, you will do best if you are thoroughly prepared, because the other person will be. They do their homework and come ready to quote statistics (legitimate or not) to prove their antigay points.

Encounters with these people are acid tests of one's ability to manage anger under pressure and stay focused and rational in the encounter. The tactic I recommend is one of "shifting the agenda." Your agenda is not to defend gay and lesbian people but to confront the homophobic person's own need to be hostile to us.

The calculating scapegoater wants us to defend because that is the more vulnerable position in any discussion. We should, instead, be in the more potent position of confronting bigotry. To illustrate the agenda-shifting tactic I offer the following scene involving a calculating scapegoater, a man who is often on television to represent the traditional family values (read antigay) point of view.

John (we'll call him) works for a Washington, D.C.–based organization that appears to have as its main objective the maligning of gay and lesbian people. John's demeanor is that of a robotic actor—only his mouth moves when he talks; his face is immobile, emotionless.

In repose, John's eyes dart from side to side, as if patrolling for danger. Occasionally he smiles a slightly demented grin which is also one of the ways he shows disdain for what his opponent is saying. More often he mutters under, or talks over, what the other person is saying.

I choose John to write about because I have watched him

on television programs push poised, intelligent, articulate gay and lesbian opponents to barely controlled rage. In his flat voice he tells outrageous lies about homosexuality and gay people. He never looks at his opponent; rather, he stares into empty space, which makes him seem inaccessible, almost not there to engage.

As he heaps contempt on everything gay, the gay or lesbian person usually begins defending, arguing, trying to correct the record. It is like running up a down escalator. You never get there.

Here is my fantasy of *your* successful encounter with John. No defending, arguing, or correcting the record on gay. The topic is *his* bigotry. The following points should be pursued no matter what his answers are. These are his actual comments on a recent television program.

John: Most people agree that homosexuality is not normal. It is demonstrably destructive as a way of life. It is dangerous, so many social pathologies—suicide, alcoholism, drug addiction, sexual aberrations—it is just a sad way to be.

You: By your distorted comments on homosexuality you are striking at the core of my identity as a human being. I think that gives me permission to question your motivation. Why are you so bent on vilifying homosexuals? What does that do for *you*?

John: I don't know what you're talking about. I am only speaking the truth about what I know to be a destructive lifestyle, full of despair and anguish.

You: What you say about gay people is demeaning and hurtful, as well as being untrue. Why do you want to hurt gay people?

John: I don't want to hurt gay people. Some of my best friends are gay. I worry about them because they are in a lot of trouble.

You: Have you always felt this way about gay people? Do you remember when you first felt this way?

John: I've always felt this way. It isn't just my judgment. It's the way most people feel about gays—always have, always will—because it's a terrible way to live. Somebody has to watch out for the young people of this country. You think it's okay to bring homosexuals into the classroom to teach that it's normal to be gay. Why not bring in drug addicts to say what good feelings one can get from drugs? It's the same thing.

You: What you are saying makes sense only in terms of your antigay agenda. What need is served for you by this condemnation of people who never did anything to you?

John: The need is to educate the American public to the dangers of promoting a dangerous lifestyle. That's all.

You: If you are indeed such a moral crusader, why do you not focus on things that pose *real* dangers to our society: crime and violence, the physical and sexual abuse of children that is epidemic in our country, homelessness and a killer drug industry. Why have you not devoted your energy to these issues?

John: How do you know I don't devote energy to these issues?

You: Because all you do when you appear on television is disparage gay people. It seems to be an obsession with you. Just what is the allure of homosexuality for you?

John: I believe homosexuality is a major threat to the stability of the American way of life. Your gay agenda is morally corrupt. You seek to convert this society to your perverse way of living. You have declared war on family values in this country and it's essential that your campaign for doing away with the heterosexual ethic be stopped.

You: John, it sounds as if homosexuality is a major threat to *your* stability. Do you understand why you are so dedicated to this absurd notion that we are out to convert you and corrupt you? Do you have any idea what's behind this concern for you?

As I wrote this, I tried to imagine what would happen if such questions were posed. Would the host of the show abort the questioning and try to get back to talking about gay and lesbian issues rather than John's bigotry? What if that happens? In my fantasy you are well prepared with the following kind of response:

> "You may believe it is legitimate to ask, 'Should gay and lesbian people have all the same rights as every other American citizen?' It is just as legitimate to address the *reasons* such a question would be asked at all.
> "The question is asked by people who do not relate to gays as being real, like them. These people cannot see beyond their stereotypes. They are captive to ideas about human nature that are thousands of years old and obsolete in a changing modern world.
> The question is asked by people struggling to combat the powerlessness in their own lives, needing a scapegoat to blame for the frustration of a flawed life.
> And the question is asked by individuals who have something to gain, personally or politically, by controlling the lives of other people. It is therefore just as legitimate to talk here about a person's prejudice and bigotry as it is to talk about homosexuality, because if it were not for prejudice and bigotry homosexuality would not be an issue. That is at the heart of the matter. You cannot turn away from that."

Pulling off this confrontation would not be easy, but it is the kind of agenda shifting that I believe is necessary to prevail over serious bigots. Actually, shifting the agenda is a tactic that can be effective in any encounter you might have with someone who is perhaps not a serious bigot but is operating out of a homophobic frame of reference nevertheless.

Let us say you are faced with a friend or relative who is well intentioned but is insisting that you *could* change if you wanted to. The subtext, of course, is that you should change because being homosexual is abnormal and undesirable. Rather than defending the normality of being gay you might focus on the aberrant aspect of wanting to hurt people you don't know, who have never done anything to you.

The same tactic can be useful in encounters where you come up against a stranger's homophobia. You could ignore the homophobic remark made, but you are tired of that cop-out. You want to respond. It doesn't feel right to be defensive. *The alternative is to shift the agenda from what is wrong with gay people to what is wrong with homophobia.*

It would not be unusual to be in a situation where you had to share not only a public space with others but the experience of being subjected to a calculating scapegoater on radio or television. Let's say you are in a bar (not a gay one) and the television is blaring forth. Rush Limbaugh is on a tirade about homosexuals wanting special rights. He characterizes gay and lesbian people in the most derogatory terms. The person sitting next to you is nodding in agreement with Limbaugh.

"You got that right, Rush," he says to the television. Then he turns to you and says, "He is right on, isn't he?"

You take a deep breath and say, "No, I think he is way off."

The man gives you a long look. "You don't agree?"

"No, I just wonder why he needs to be so angry at gay people."

"He's not angry. He's just saying it like it is. I happen to agree with him."

"What is the payoff for you in condemning people you know nothing about?"

"It's not about me, it's about them."

"No, it's about you and your opinion of gay people, which sounds like a prejudice that you learned somewhere."

At this point a variety of things could happen. Your adversary could turn away and ignore you, he could leave, or he could really get into the conversation, arguing with you or possibly even questioning his own assumption that everyone does agree with him and Rush.

What is important is how *you* feel having taken a stand in a difficult situation. No matter how the scenario plays out, you have achieved a quiet victory. Just being able to address the homophobia issue with someone who would rather say negative things about gay people, you are claiming your right to a voice in the debate.

It is no small task to pull the cover on ignorance, hatred, and the blind faith of true believers. No one wants to admit to these things, but the reality is that these are the motivating factors enabling some good, some terrible people to sit in judgment of the lives of gay and lesbian Americans and to scapegoat our community in the service of their own self-validation.

It is essential to uncover this reality. Until we start talking about unexamined prejudices, the need to scapegoat, and the irrationality of aggressing against total strangers, we will be at the mercy of both well-intentioned but homophobic Cousin Suzy, and the calculating scapegoaters who reinforce her erroneous ideas about what moral behavior is.

The important thing is to keep in mind that gay and lesbian people have done nothing wrong. When we are under attack it is because the attacker has either an internal agenda or a practical objective to take care of. It is about them, not us. It is their house that is disordered. They need to feel personally validated. Or they need to whip the masses into submission, into giving money and providing votes. Either way, theirs is a self-serving agenda and we do not need to be co-opted by it.

We must try not to *internalize* their distorted ideas about who and what we are. We must not back off and leave them in charge of the forum. We need to be heard and seen and understood. We have to do that for ourselves. We have to use our energy to illuminate the truth. That is what this book is about—how to join the battle where it belongs—talking about *them*, exposing those wellsprings of hate and bigotry that drive both skinheads and United States senators to victimize us in order to get their fix of power.

6

True Morality and the Moral Dilemma

The religious right likes to talk about morality. What they say is that homosexuals are immoral, or that we have no morals. What they mean is that homosexuals are different from them. Heterosexual is moral; anything different is immoral. The simplistic nature of this assertion is obvious, but not to the millions of right-wing Christians who follow their leaders with mindless devotion, and parrot their pronouncements with evangelical zeal.

However, you don't have to be a right-wing Christian to be convinced that gay and lesbian people are somehow morally impaired. You just have to be one of those many people who confuse morality with conformity. There may be members of your own family who love you but can't understand why you have to live this "immoral" gay life. What they mean is this life that doesn't conform to the familiar conventions by which *they* live.

Because "morality" *is* so much a staple of the religious right's rhetoric, I think it is important to understand how *true*

morality actually develops, how people do become moral beings. It is essential to make a distinction here between two in-
terpretations of what morality is—one based on intrinsic
experience, the other on religious dogma.

First, there is a person's ability to distinguish right from
wrong, and proceed, or not, with an action, knowing the difference. That is about the morality of individual human beings. It
is an intrinsic experience of moral judgment.

Then, there is religious dogma that puts forth "rules for living"—a preestablished code of conduct that demands strict
conformity. Morality in this instance is defined by how closely
one conforms to this code of conduct, which may or may not be
relevant to a given time, place, or population.

Conformity is often mistaken for morality, and this error is
at the heart of the assertion that homosexuals are "immoral."
People who are homosexual do not conform to the traditional
male/female social program. We are nonconforming and that is
supposed to make us immoral.

What we are interested in here is true morality, not conformity to a code, or tradition, or religious dogma, but the ability
of an individual to decide what is right or wrong behavior, particularly as it regards other human beings. This ability begins to
develop at an early age, but changes in specific ways as the individual moves toward maturity. The process of an evolving moral
sense has been systematically studied by psychologists and soci-
ologists for years.

Of all the behavioral scientists who have looked at how
moral reasoning develops, Lawrence Kohlberg's work has been
the most influential. While this continues to be true, mention
should also be made here of the work of Carol Gilligan, who, in
her book (*In a Different Voice*), has elaborated Kohlberg's theory to highlight the experiences of women. The studies on
which Kohlberg's ideas are based included only male subjects.

Gilligan makes the point, among others, that girls are so-
cialized differently from boys. In particular, boys are defined
more by how well they separate from parents and become *inde-*

pendent and *competitive*. Girls are more relationship oriented and are defined by how well they are able to form and be sensitive to the *attachments* in their lives. How this might affect the differences in their moral development I will comment on below.

The following is a simplified interpretation of Kohlberg's theory and its implications.

Moral Development in Human Beings

Kohlberg divides a person's life into three developmental periods (once past the earliest years):

Ages four to ten years,
Ages ten to thirteen years,
Ages thirteen years to young adulthood.

Level One (Ages Four to Ten)

In this period, morality—whether behavior is right or wrong—is judged according to outcome. The child wishes to avoid punishment; therefore, what does not get punished is right and what does get punished is wrong. The important thing is to figure out how *not* to get punished.

In a later stage of this period, actions are considered right if they produce what the person wants (outcome), and wrong if they do not produce what the person wants. It's all a matter of practicality, with little or no concern for the needs of anyone else.

People who progress no further in their moral development than this level tend to become antisocial adults who do not consider the effect of their actions on others because they are interested only in getting their own needs met. These adults are the truly amoral people since their development has not incorporated the shared concepts of right and wrong that most of us live by—concepts that do take into account the needs and wishes of the people around us.

"What can I get away with?" is the question that often shapes decisions about what actions to take for the level one adult. Life is a game of strategizing one's way around the rules, using people to accomplish objectives that have meaning only to the user.

In the case of the person whose moral development is fore-closed at level one, the cause is often the inability of parent figures to allow separation from their influence, which keeps the individual thinking in terms of parental punishment or the avoidance of it. These parent figures are likely to be strict disciplinarians, binding their child to them so that outside influences, crucial to the development of moral *maturity*, cannot compete.

Another condition producing level one adults is the absence of parenting altogether because there is no family, either in spirit, or in fact. Lacking adequate guidance, this person grows up without a moral compass, unable to distinguish right from wrong except as a vehicle for self-gratification.

Level Two (Ages Ten to Thirteen)

In this period, right and wrong are judged according to whether or not the adults in one's life are pleased and show approval of an action. Approval means it's right. Disapproval means it's wrong. A lifelong pattern is established in which morality is determined by what other people think of one's behavior.

In a later stage of this period emphasis is on following the rules with a tendency to see rules and laws as fixed and unchangeable (as many people see the Bible). External authority is all-important, as is conforming to what are perceived as the expectations of most people—the rule of the majority.

Here there might be one of the important differences in the way women develop as opposed to men. For women the "rules of the game" tend not to be so important as they are for men. Women are likely to be guided more in their dealings with others by the quality of the relationship involved. There may be just as much followership by women at this level but it will be influenced more by whom they relate to than by strict adherence to a set of rules.

People who do not progress in their development beyond this level tend to become, as adults, the followers, the true believers, individuals who are suspicious of anyone who is different from them—who doesn't follow the crowd. Level two people are the traditionalists, who resist change and mistrust anyone who seems to want to bring about change.

Level two people are the best candidates for any demagogue who can pull off a credible show of authority. Extreme examples are cult members such as those who surrendered their individual judgment to Jim Jones in the Jonestown tragedy, and the people who lived, and died, with David Koresh in the Branch Davidian compound in Waco, Texas.

Less extreme are the level two adults who respond to the likes of Pat Robertson who tell them that they must follow his lead or the nation will "continue to legalize sodomy, slaughter innocent babies, destroy the minds of her children, squander her resources and sink into oblivion!" He sounds the alarm and level two people follow his lead.

When Pat Robertson tells his vast Christian Broadcasting Network audience to flood Congress and the White House with letters and phone calls, they do as they are told, seeing themselves as warriors saving the "soul of America." Pat Robertson gets richer and more politically powerful, and bigotry, disguised as patriotism, is celebrated, reinforced, and exploited.

These are the people for whom conformity to a code of conduct, to tradition, and to religious dogma constitutes "morality." They are redeemed from their own spiritual inertia by joining Pat Robertson's fantasy war against the forces of evil—predatory homosexuals out to steal their children and destroy American family life.

Or, to be less extreme about it, these are also people who have simply grown up in a conservative environment and take their comfort from the conviction that their parents were right and they will be okay if they just hew to the values they were taught as children. The fact that the world is changing around them seems to have little impact.

This level two adult may even be good old Aunt Judith whose interest in your wayward "lifestyle" is about your spiritual redemption—at least that's what she thinks. Her security in life rests on the mistaken premise that traditional is the same as natural. You had better stick with the traditional, she believes, because you certainly wouldn't want to end up being "unnatural."

Level Three (Ages Thirteen to Young Adulthood)

In this period, right and wrong are judged not according to what others think but according to *internal* criteria—personal decisions based on ethical principles evolved from the lessons of life. Moral judgments take into account such things as the circumstances of an action and the rights of the individuals involved.

Laws are seen as changeable when the needs and standards of the society change. The slaves were freed. Women got the vote. Interracial marriage was decriminalized. Abortion was legalized. Segregation was outlawed. Sexual harassment became a crime.

Level three moral reasoning utilizes the universal principles of justice, equality of human rights, and respect for the dignity of individuals in making judgments about what is right or wrong. Morality is not conformity, it is concern for others, openness to their individuality, and the willingness to behave responsibly and ethically toward them no matter how different from you they may be.

A variation in the way women develop moral judgment at this point would involve an emphasis for women on caring and responsibility in relationships as a basis for moral behavior rather than the male's emphasis on attention to fairness, human rights, and principles of justice. Even though the causative elements may be somewhat different for women and men at level three, the effect of willingness to behave responsibly and consult internal criteria in making moral judgments would be the same.

This is moral maturity—the ability to think for oneself, not just depend upon outside sources to dictate what is right and wrong. Moral maturity always includes an openness to learning and changing, a commitment to human rights, and respect for individual differences. The "morality" that the religious right talks about is a far cry from the understanding of moral maturity that has emerged from many years of behavioral science research.

The Christian Right and Morality

The morality celebrated in the Christian right's rhetoric is that typical of level two, the ages ten to thirteen period of moral development, in which judgments are made to conform to the attitudes of the majority rather than taking into account the needs of the individuals involved. For instance, to a person foreclosed at this stage of moral development, the personal lives and civil rights of gay men and lesbians in this country are virtually without meaning. What counts is the perception of agreeing with "what most people think"—being of the majority.

This inclination of the homophobes to try to keep gays and lesbians invisible as real people reinforces the notion that we are an odd little group of misfits who *deserve* to be marginalized by society. Every time a gay or lesbian person comes out of the closet it gets a little harder to ignore our existence as ordinary human beings. Coming out is our most powerful weapon against discrimination.

For the adult whose moral development does not progress

past level two, where external authority is all-important, notions of right and wrong are likely to come from what the Bible
says, or what is heard from the pulpit, the authority of each to
remain unchallenged.

There is little or no openness to new learning for these individuals. Personal security is predicated on a sureness that conforming to the code of conduct followed by the majority of
like-minded people insures that life will be righteous, sancti-
fied, and beyond reproach. Morality for these people is essentially about conformity.

The Moral Dilemma

So, how does anyone progress from one level of moral development to the next? For children, at level one, the move out of
the family into the larger world of school and friends downplays
the importance of parental reward and punishment as the sole
basis for knowing what is right or wrong. Emphasis shifts to a
more complicated process of figuring out how to please the *variety* of peers and adults in one's life.

Since the expectations of many of these different people
are likely to be in conflict with one another, a *moral dilemma* occurs. Whom to follow? What to believe? How to behave? It is
this *moral dilemma* that causes the individual to question previously held beliefs, open up to new ideas, and have the opportunity to move beyond the restraints of level one to the broader
involvement with the world of level two.

A typical example of a teenage dilemma that would move
the individual from level one to level two would be contradic-
tory pressures from home and from peers. Parents warn against
promiscuous sex, and drug and alcohol use. Peers endorse having sex (everybody's doing it) and pressure friends to be one of
the gang getting high on alcohol and trying drugs. The
dilemma produced is in how to integrate the contradiction be-

tween what would please parents and what would please peers. The dilemma moves the adolescent out of level one.

For teenagers, in level two, questioning beliefs, standards, and values is everyday stuff since adolescence is primarily an ongoing crisis of identity. To make sense of an ever-changing self-perception the teenager must continually discard, modify, and take on new beliefs about right and wrong behavior.

This is the moral dilemma of level two that forces, for most people, development of a set of internal ethical principles based not on what the majority dictates but on the changing reality of one's own life. The dilemma moves one toward integration of conflicting influences.

If this transition occurs successfully, these individuals progress to level three of their moral development, which necessarily includes acknowledgment that the world is a complex collection of diverse human beings from whom one does not live in isolation. Therefore there cannot be one set of standards for all, nor can there be a single authority able to dictate how diverse people should live.

If a moral dilemma is the precipitating factor in enabling a person to move from one level of moral development to another, what is the fate of prejudiced individuals foreclosed at level two—locked into biblical authority and the tyranny of majority thinking as the basis of morality? What moral dilemma—what conflict of values—might shake up their belief system?

Two situations come to mind. The first is what we have learned from the struggle for racial integration in this country. Proximity and association in the schools, in the military, and in the workplace have created the opportunity for people of different races to relate to one another as human beings rather than as stereotypes.

For many, the moral dilemma of whether or not to cling to the old views, and relate to these individuals in the abstract, has come into conflict with the natural inclination of people to respond altruistically when daily contact is inevitable. This conflict requires a reexamination of one's prejudices, and often produces a positive shift in how people perceive one another.

The situation that typically generates a moral dilemma for people with antigay prejudices is the discovery that someone they work with and like, someone they know and admire, or someone they are related to and love, is gay or lesbian. Then there is the conflict of whether to foreclose on a valued relationship or let go of the safety of conforming thought and be willing to question their own prejudices. It is this kind of moral dilemma that can turn a homophobic colleague, friend, or relative into a supporter, if not a champion, of gay and lesbian rights.

Take, for instance, the case of Alan Schindler, the American sailor brutally murdered by a homophobic shipmate in Japan. Dorothy Hajdys, his mother, initially vehemently denied that her son even was homosexual, but the moral dilemma precipitated by learning how and why he was murdered brought her to a reexamination of her beliefs. It was a transforming experience. Only months later, Dorothy Hajdys was speaking to a television audience of millions in support of gay rights at the 1993 Lesbian and Gay March on Washington.

Then there is Marie Pridgen, mother of a gay man beaten in a North Carolina bar in January 1993 by U.S. Marines furious over President Clinton's announcement that he intended to lift the ban on gays in the military. Marie Pridgen had previously been so distressed over her son's homosexuality that she had taken to hauling him out of gay bars and had forced him to enroll in a program to become an "ex-gay."

The moral dilemma produced by encountering the vicious homophobia that had victimized her child caused her to question her own prejudices. By April 1993 she was walking the corridors of the United States Capitol with her son, lobbying members of Congress to admit openly gay men and women to the armed forces. She had become a fighter for ending the antigay discrimination that had once motivated her own behavior.

The most poignant example of a parent whose moral

dilemma enabled a drastic shift in attitude and behavior is that of Mary Griffin, a devout Christian fundamentalist who badgered and berated her son Bobby for being gay until, no longer able to stand the pressure, he climbed over the railing of a highway overpass and jumped to his death.

Mary Griffin has since turned the story of her tragedy into a powerful wake-up call, traveling and lecturing, imploring the parents of lesbians and gays to understand and accept their children while they still have a chance.

Th experiences of these mothers are in the extreme. One should not have to lose a child, or even have one beaten up, as a prelude to examining antigay prejudices. It should be enough just to learn that a son is gay, or a daughter is lesbian. The point is that every time a gay man or lesbian comes out, there is the potential for anyone in that person's environment to become conflicted enough to examine his or her antigay prejudice, and, possibly, make the transition to a more mature level of moral reasoning.

Hopefully, an understanding of the true meaning of morality can help to put in perspective the absurd accusations of the homophobes about the "morality" of gay and lesbian people. Understanding how moral reasoning develops should also provide insight into the moral *immaturity* of those individuals whose judgments of what is right and wrong are determined by what they think they are supposed to believe in order to earn the acceptance of their peers.

Part II——Finding Solutions

7

There's More Than One Way to Respond

It would be foolish to think that every gay or lesbian person is going to be able to, or even want to, respond to encounters with bigotry in the same way. The "old pro" lesbian or gay man who has been out and an activist for twenty years is likely to react quite differently from the young person who has barely come out and is still struggling with what it all means.

The shy individual will have a different problem with responding to bigotry than the outgoing, gregarious person. The self-employed gay or lesbian is likely to feel less the need to be cautious about what he or she says than the person who depends for his or her income on being in the good graces of an employer. Those who must struggle with the dual oppression of being gay or lesbian and a member of an ethnic or racial minority will have different issues to deal with from their nonminority counterparts.

Bigotry encountered in the supermarket checkout line is different from antigay prejudice encountered in one's own family or workplace. Where one is physically located at the time of experiencing a bigoted act should determine how much of a risk it is wise to take. There is no *one way* to stand up to bigotry.

Following is a series of vignettes illustrating different ways of responding in encounters with bigotry. I have classified them according to three categories:

Personalizing—It's *Me* You're Talking About
Educating—This Is How It is
Vindicating—When Action Speaks Louder Than Words

Personalizing

Here the emphasis is on forcing the other person to see that antigay remarks may be hurting someone present, even someone he or she cares about.

Friends

Marty and John had been friends for years. Though they disagreed about a lot of things, they considered themselves close. Marty had come out to John some time ago but they tended not to talk much about Marty's life. Occasionally John would say something homophobic but Marty chose to ignore these remarks, not wanting to hurt the relationship.

One day John was sounding off about an article he'd seen in the newspaper about gay men and lesbians having children. He said that this was too much for him. He believed in live and let live, but children should be raised by regular moms and dads, not homosexuals. Marty could feel the anger rising in him. He tried to push it down but this time it didn't work.

Suddenly it was not just the relationship that Marty was thinking about. He felt stung by the remark about gays as parents. Some of his gay and lesbian friends were parents and he knew how devoted and loving they were with their children. Something shifted for Marty. He had always protected his friendship with John in his own mind, but now the risk of losing

John's approval seemed secondary to confronting the homophobia that he could no longer ignore.

"John, you are such a great guy but you seem to have this problem with gay. Why is that? You like people, you're friendly, you're open, except when it comes to gays. You puzzle me."

John denied that there was anything unusual about his attitude. He said it was the way most people feel, especially when it comes to children. Marty reminded John that he, Marty, was gay and when John was trashing gay people he was trashing him. John tried to wiggle out of this connection but Marty persisted, realizing he shouldn't have let John get away with so much for so long and promising himself that he would not ignore John's homophobic remarks in the future.

Marty found that gentle persuasion worked best on John. Every time John said anything even vaguely homophobic, Marty quietly reminded him that he was taking it personally. Eventually, John started to *catch himself* about to say something antigay around Marty. As this was happening, he began to see how easy it was to run down strangers and how different it felt when someone you knew and cared about was affected.

Fags Are Not Real Men

Tyrell had wanted to be a police officer ever since he was a little boy. He grew up in South Central Los Angeles, surrounded by the temptations of easy drug money, the lure of gangs, and people who were convinced that the police were the enemy. In spite of all this he never wavered in his ambition to be a cop, though he was wise enough not to talk about it with his peers.

After high school, Tyrell went to two years of city college, then applied for and got a job working for the Los Angeles Police Department. Tyrell loved it all, the training, the patrols, the camaraderie with his fellow officers. He was a good cop and in his first few years he received a number of commendations for his performance on the street.

One day Tyrell was told that he was going on special assignment, to the vice squad. He was to work the gay bookstores un-
dercover and if he was approached for sex he was to make an
arrest. Tyrell felt nervous about this assignment. He didn't like
the idea of arresting gay men, because he himself was gay, though
he had not discussed this with anyone in the department. He
lived a double life, being just another macho cop by day, and
moving in the world of gay bars and friendships at night.

Tyrell had thought that being gay never had to come out
because it had nothing to do with his police work. Suddenly it
was having too much to do with it. Every time Tyrell went into
a gay bookstore his head was reeling with thoughts about betrayal. He was betraying himself by pretending to be straight.
He was betraying gay men by luring them into danger. He felt
terrible about what he was doing.

One day Tyrell was hanging around one of the stores when a
man came in who Tyrell had picked up in a bar once. The man
seemed glad to see him and quietly suggested they go into a
booth together. Tyrell panicked. If he arrested this guy his cover
might be blown. He could always deny that he knew him, but
he wasn't sure what the man remembered about him. He felt
confused and the only solution seemed to be retreat. He stammered that he had to go and hastily left the store.

Tyrell had dealt with the bookstore situation but he was left
with an uneasy feeling. He told himself that he had been smart
to run away but it felt like he was cheating all around—the poor
guy in the store, his job, and most of all himself. He suddenly
felt very lonely, as if he couldn't be real anywhere. His friends
didn't know about the work he was doing. His superiors didn't
know he was gay. And he was now living in fear of being discovered by practically everyone around him.

"Wait a minute," he told himself. "I have to think about
some options here. I do have friends on the force. If I can just
think who I would trust at least I'd have someone to talk to.
Everybody doesn't have to know. Who do I really trust?"

Tyrell thought about how good it would feel to be able to be

himself with even a few people. He picked the two fellow officers he was closest to, Martin and Gary, both of whom he'd
gone through the police academy with.

Gary was startled at Tyrell's revelation, but he said, "Hey
man, you're the same person, so what?" But Martin was another
story. He quietly nodded and said, "Okay," and that was all.

Tyrell was particularly close to Martin's wife, Adina, who often invited him to dinner with the comment that a bachelor
needed a good home-cooked meal once in a while.

One night Tyrell and Adina were waiting for Martin to come
home. When he finally came in it was clear that he was drunk.
Martin immediately went to the kitchen cabinet where the
liquor was kept and poured himself a stiff drink. Tyrell laughed
and said, "Man, you have got a snootful. Maybe you ought to
knock it off."

Martin glared at Tyrell. "Oh, so that's what you think. Well,
you would because fags don't understand what real men do, because fags are *not* real men."

Tyrell felt shocked. He looked quickly at Adina, who looked
pained though he wasn't sure if it was because he'd been outed
or because of her husband's rudeness.

Tyrell smiled. "Come on, Martin. What do you mean, not
real men? We went through the academy together. I did everything you did. And I've got more commendations than you do.
What's a *real man* anyway? I'm real, brother, and right now I'm
pissed at what you're saying. Why are you doing this?"

Martin just stared at Tyrell. "I don't know. I just don't like
fags and I don't like that you're one of them."

Tyrell said in a steady voice, "Martin, I'm the same guy
you've known for years. What you're saying hurts me, big-time.
I don't understand why you're doing this now."

Martin sat down heavily. He seemed weary. "I don't know. I
just had to get it out. Whatever."

Tyrell sat down across from Martin. "Listen to me. We can
talk about this, any time, but don't do *this* again. It hurts, see?
Don't do it again."

Adina put her hand on Tyrell's shoulder. "I think it's time to get some food into all of us."

In the days following, Martin avoided Tyrell until they came face-to-face as Martin was leaving the station and Tyrell was entering. Martin stopped, looking as if he wanted to say something. He just stood in front of Tyrell, not speaking. Finally, Martin put out his hand.

"I didn't want to hurt you. I'm just trying to figure this out."

"Me too, pal. I'm trying to figure it out too. Just don't make it harder by attacking me."

Martin nodded. "It isn't you, it's this thing."

Tyrell looked Martin in the eye. "No, that's what you have to understand. It *is* me. It's me you're talking about and it's my feelings I'm asking you to deal with."

Tyrell felt good about being able to personalize the issue for Martin, as he had personalized it for himself when he requested a transfer off his vice-squad assignment.

In the Supermarket

Shirley wheeled her basket into the supermarket checkout line and pulled a magazine out of the rack. Just in the process of coming out, Shirley was no longer comfortable with hiding who she was, yet she was not ready to announce to the world at large that she was a lesbian. As she leafed through the magazine she inadvertently tuned into the conversation of the two women behind her in line. They were discussing the bag boy.

"Look at that earring in his ear. He must be one of those, you know"—her voice trailed off into a whisper—"*queers.*"

Her friend responded, "Oh yes, they're everywhere you look these days. It's a terrible example for young kids. They shouldn't have him working here."

Shirley felt the anger rising in her but she continued to stare into her magazine.

"Don't you pity that boy's poor mother? She must be embarrassed to have a son like that."

Shirley told herself that it would be pointless to confront these old biddies, that she wasn't going to educate them, that she would probably just make a fool of herself. Why risk that?

One of the women nudged the other and gave her limp wrist a little shake. Both giggled.

Shirley snapped the magazine closed. She took a deep breath and turned to face the two women.

"Excuse me, I couldn't help but overhear what you were saying. You don't know that he's gay just because he wears an earring. And if he is gay, so what? Does that make him unfit to bag your groceries? How silly. Isn't that silly?" Both women shot hostile glances at Shirley.

"If he is gay and wants to show it he is a terrific *example* of someone who feels good about himself . . . and his mother probably had a lot to do with it by loving him as he is. Think about that."

The women turned away from Shirley, who was now wound up enough to continue talking at their backs.

"Your judgments are not only prejudiced, they're hurtful." One woman turned and glared at Shirley. She said in a defiant tone, "We didn't mean any harm."

"Maybe you didn't mean any harm but frankly *I* feel harmed because the things you're saying about him apply to me and to every other gay person."

The woman stared at Shirley, speechless. Shirley felt a surge of excitement as she met the woman's eyes.

"You might think about what happened here the next time you feel like making fun of a gay person."

The two women moved quickly toward the door. Shirley smiled, and mentally gave herself a pat on the back.

At the Fast-Food Counter

It was midafternoon when Ernie stopped for lunch. There were few people in the fast-food restaurant. Ernie had ordered from the counterperson and he stepped aside while he waited for his food. As the person behind him moved up to order, Ernie saw the counterman whisper something to the fellow working next to him, and then they both rolled their eyes and giggled.

Looking around to see what was so funny, Ernie noticed a decidedly effeminate young man standing in a nearby line. When he looked back to the guys behind the counter it was apparent that they were laughing at the young man. Ernie wanted to leap over the counter and bang their heads together. He calmed himself down and thought about what to do.

Ernie was Latino, as were the men behind the counter. He'd had his run-ins with gay-bashers from his own ethnic community in the past. Even his own brothers had trouble with his being gay. He was reminded in this moment of how much he was hurt by his brothers' disapproval.

Suddenly it all came together for him. When his food was ready he leaned over the counter and said, "What were you laughing at?"

The counterman did a double take. "Nothing. I don't know what you're talking about."

"I saw you and this other guy laughing. Are you making fun of that young man over there?"

The counterman fixed Ernie with a blank look, then said in a confidential tone, "Well he is a little weird."

"Then I guess you'd laugh at me too." Ernie couldn't believe he'd really said that.

"No, why would I?"

"Because I'm gay and you probably think I'm weird too."

The counterman was silent.

Ernie was warming up now. "A lot of your customers might be gay. Is this the way you are going to treat them—calling them weird and laughing at them. I think your supervisor would like to know about that."

The counterman looked confused, as if he didn't quite understand what was happening.

"Look, chill out man. I'm sorry. He just looked weird to me. It has nothing to do with you."

Ernie felt his anger coming up again. "You don't seem to get it. It has everything to do with me because I'm gay and when you make fun of him you make fun of me. And with that Ernie suddenly realized that he need not go on with this poor guy, who now looked frightened as well as bewildered.

Ernie had not let this person get away with ridiculing the young man. He had made an honest statement about himself, and he believed he had gotten through—at least his threat about the supervisor had. He gave the counterman one last evil look and moved off, feeling quite satisfied with himself.

Educating

The following vignettes are about simple acts of educating—this is how it is. While the other person may not have meant to be hurtful, their antigay prejudice is revealed in what they do.

The Wedding Picture

Marilyn and Jane were guests at the wedding of Jane's cousin, Phillip. Having had an elaborate Holy Union ceremony to seal their own commitment to each other, they were happy to be sharing this special time with Phillip and his bride.

The wedding was beautiful and Marilyn and Jane felt warmed by the affection and happiness that seemed to permeate the occasion. After the ceremony the family gathered in a side room for photos before going into the reception. Jane's Aunt Agatha was busily talking to the photographer about how the pictures would be set up.

When everyone had arrived Aunt Aggie beckoned people to the front of the room. She called for the children to sit down in front and the adult relatives and their spouses to stand behind.

"C'mon, Jane. You're in the family picture!" Aunt Aggie

shouted. Jane waited to hear Marilyn's name called. All she heard was, "C'mon, Jane, you're holding everything up."

Marilyn and Jane looked at each other. Marilyn said, "Go on, you're holding everything up."

Jane couldn't believe this was happening. She told herself that it was an oversight, that Aunt Agatha had *meant* Jane and Marilyn when she said "Jane." But once again her aunt shouted, "Come *on*, Jane."

Jane felt confused. She wasn't sure if she should say something, but she felt too shy to make a scene, and it would have been one if she said what she was thinking. Suddenly she just wanted to be out of there. She took Marilyn's hand and led her out of the room.

At the reception afterward Aunt Aggie approached Jane.

"What is wrong with you, girl? Why didn't you want to be in the family picture?"

"Aunt Aggie, you know my partner, Marilyn?"

"Well of course I do. How are you, dear?"

Jane took a deep breath. "Aunt Aggie, Marilyn was not invited to be in the picture with everyone else's spouses so I chose not to be in the picture either."

Aunt Aggie looked confused. "But, it was the *family* picture, just the family."

Jane realized that she had been trying to protect Aunt Agatha in her own mind. It wasn't an oversight, it was what she feared it was.

"Look, Auntie, Marilyn is as much a part of the family as Susan's husband, and Morris's wife, and Uncle Joe's dear old Emily. She is my partner in life just as Susan's Alex is her partner in life."

Aunt Aggie looked as if she suddenly got it.

"Janie, I never thought. I just didn't think. I wouldn't hurt either one of you for the world. Marilyn, can you ever forgive me?"

Marilyn smiled. "I forgive you, Aggie."

"Janie?"

Jane felt as if she really wanted to say no, that she did not forgive such an offense, but Aunt Aggie looked so contrite she decided to forgo self-indulgence and let her aunt off the hook.

"I think you've got the message, Aunt Aggie, and I hope something like this won't happen again. Marilyn *is* our family."

"It won't happen again, girls, I promise."

Jane wondered how old they would have to get before Aggie stopped calling them "girls," but she decided to let that one go for another time.

Being Hit On

Being African-American, Violet felt it was always important to walk proud, to say with her every movement that she was glad she was who she was. In college, Violet finally came to terms with being a lesbian, and she rewarded herself by falling in love and beginning a relationship that felt as if she had come home at last.

Violet and Angie were attractive black young women. When they were in public together it was not unusual for men to hit on them. Usually they just politely declined all come-ons and that was that. Occasionally, however, they encountered a man who wouldn't take no for an answer.

On this particular night Violet and Angie were out to dinner. There were four black men at a nearby table. Violet and Angie were aware that these men were talking about them, glancing in their direction, obviously enjoying whatever observations they were making. Suddenly one of the men pushed his chair back and headed toward them. He was a little drunk, apparent from the abrupt stop he made in front of them, as if he hadn't expected the distance to be quite so short.

The man said he was sorry to interrupt but he was so taken with two such beautiful women that he just had to come over and see if they'd like to join him and his friends. Violet said no thank you and turned back to her dinner. The man shrugged and left. But in a few minutes he was back asking again for their company. Violet felt annoyed. Her voice had an edge to it as she said again, "No thank you." Now the man seemed really determined to achieve his purpose. He came back again and this time his proposal grew more insistent and aggressive. He said that he accepted that they didn't want to join his friends but how about the three of them having some fun.

Violet's fury was apparent from the look in her eyes. She felt like punching this guy but she was acutely aware that she and Angie were in a potentially risky situation. Nevertheless, she sat very straight in her chair and said in a firm voice, "Look, we are together, very together—we are a couple. Nothing personal, but we aren't into anything with anyone else. So thank you, but no thank you."

"You know what you girls need. . . ."

Angie too was struggling with her feelings. She felt a little frightened but she said in a determinedly calm voice, "Yes, we know, we need for you to hear what we're saying. It's not about you. It's about us. We want to be alone. Now, please give us the respect we've given you, so far."

Angie stared directly into the man's eyes as she emphasized the "so far."

"Dykes," the man muttered.

Angie smiled. "That's right. You've understood at last. Thank you."

The man hesitated, then backed away. Grimacing, he turned and walked quickly back to his table. As he huddled with his friends they all shook their heads as they stole glances at the two women. Very soon they became immersed in their own conversation. The forays to Violet and Angie's table were over.

The Family Tree

It had been some years since I'd seen Uncle Harry, my mother's only brother and her last surviving sibling from a family of six. Uncle Harry was a retired engineer and he lived quietly with his wife in the noisy city of Las Vegas.

A bombardier in the Army Air Corps, Harry had returned from World War II visibly subdued—terribly affected, I thought, by the ruination he'd been a part of. He was a rough-around-the-edges guy with a sweet temperament and a droll sense of humor which fully emerged once the effects of the war began to fade.

I hadn't known that Uncle Harry's hobby was genealogy when he called me recently to ask if I happened to know what year my parents had been divorced. I figured it out for him and he promised to send me a copy of the family tree he was currently working on.

A few weeks later a large envelope arrived containing a blueprint that folded out and out and out to reveal aunts, uncles, cousins, marriages, divorces, births, and deaths. Not being particularly close to my family, there were many people I'd never met, but it was fascinating to follow the branches that connected wives to husbands to wives to children and their spouses and their children.

It was fun until I came to my name. The little box containing it hung out there in midair, nothing to connect me to anyone, an isolate, alone, forsaken. Wait a minute. I'm not alone. I have been in a loving relationship with a woman for twenty-two years. That is longer than any of my own parents' marriages, or my sister's marriages, or those of some of the numerous cousins I was becoming acquainted with through our family tree.

Apparently there was no place in Uncle Harry's thinking for two women to share a life, even though he had met my lover and knew we continued to be together. Our relationship had no existence for him. Quite obviously I had to do something about this.

I had no reason to believe that Harry was homophobic. I was sure it just never entered his mind to include my relationship since it wasn't a *marriage to a man*. That was what he understood, the familiarity of tradition, the predictability of convention. What he didn't understand was the variation on the theme, the nontraditional reality of same-sex love and relationship.

I pondered my strategy since I didn't want to hurt this nice man, though I did have to set him straight. My letter went like this:

> Dear Uncle Harry,
>
> Thank you for sending the family genealogy. I found it to be very interesting especially since many of these cousins I've never met or haven't seen since they were babies. Too bad there have been so many divorces and deaths and your son is the only one left to carry on the family name. Hopefully some day women will not have to take on a new identity when they marry and they can share the responsibility of preserving the family name.
>
> You really did a good job on the genealogy. There's just one problem with it. You show everyone's spouse (present and past) but you don't show mine. I have shared my life in a loving relationship with a spouse for twenty-two years but where is she on the family tree? Surely, you just forgot her because I know you wouldn't purposely deny the validity of a partnership that is at the center of my life and has endured for so long.
>
> Everyone in the family who has met Terry over the years seems to consider her family. I know you will want to do the same. When you next redo the family tree I look forward to seeing in the box below, and connected to, mine the name of Teresa DeCrescenzo, born April 18, 1944, partner to Betty Berzon since June 2, 1973.
>
> I hope you and Ida are well. Love . . .

The answer came back surprisingly quickly. Another large envelope with a blueprint that folded out and out and out. It was a revised family tree in which, indeed, Terry had a little box connected to mine with the exact wording I had suggested. A note from Uncle Harry was attached to the new family tree:

> Dear Betty and Terry,
>   When you get to the age of eighty you're not as accurate as you should be. My apology to you and Terry for the serious discrepancy. The blueprint enclosed has all the errors corrected. Other family members will also receive the revised genealogy. I hope you and Terry are in good health. Affectionately . . . Uncle Harry.

Vindicating

There are times when words fail or face-to-face discussion is impossible, when taking action is the best recourse. Here the emphasis is on sending the message: "You're mistaken if you think gay people can always be pushed around."

The Good Samaritan

It was Gay Pride Sunday in West Hollywood. The mood was festive and the streets were jammed. The parade was soon to start and people were milling about greeting friends, hugging one another, and feeling the exuberance of the day.

Paul and several of his friends decided to stop in the 7-Eleven for a cold drink before the parade. As they were coming out of the store they heard someone shouting in an angry voice. In the parking lot a man was holding a young woman by the hair, slapping her and screaming obscenities in her face. Their relationship was obvious from what was being said. She was, or had been, his girlfriend.

Paul stopped. His first impulse was to interfere but something inside told him: Be cautious. He watched for a minute while the woman sobbed and tried to pull away from her attacker. Paul could feel the tension building in him. He told himself this was none of his business, but he couldn't turn away. The woman's cries began to feel as if they were coming from inside his own head. He tried to blot out the picture in his mind of his father shouting angrily at his mother and shaking her.

Paul's friends were moving around the couple and they urged him to follow, but he felt rooted to the spot. The man hit the woman again and without thinking this time Paul went to the man and shouted at him, "Stop it! You're hurting her!"

The man let go of the woman and turned to Paul.

"Shut up you fucking faggot!"

Paul stood his ground. "If you have a problem with gay people, buddy, you're in the wrong neighborhood on the wrong day."

The man turned and put his face very close to Paul's. Paul felt the same rush of fear he had felt when his father confronted him.

"Yeah, I have a problem with fags. I hate fags. Now get out of my way you little cocksucker."

Paul didn't move. "Just leave her alone. I don't care what she is to you. No one deserves to be treated like that."

"What are you, some kind of fag hero? Nobody needs you here."

Paul thought that someone did indeed need him. He couldn't just walk away. He moved cautiously around the man and approached the woman.

"Are you all right?"

The woman gave Paul a long look, then turned her gaze to the man who was glaring at her. She turned back to Paul and said, "Shut up you fucking faggot!"

The man was laughing as he turned to the woman and slapped her again. Paul felt too startled to say anything. For a minute he couldn't move at all. Gradually he realized that words were not going to work in this situation. He knew he should move on but he was unwilling to be intimidated, especially on this of all days.

Paul walked to the telephone on the corner, dialed the sheriff's department, and reported that a woman was being beaten up by a man in front of the 7-Eleven. Within minutes the sheriff's deputies had arrived and had the man in handcuffs. As they put him in the patrol car Paul felt his tension disappear. He tried to shake the whole scene from his head as he went to rejoin his friends, who were relieved to see him.

"Well, here comes the fag hero," they chanted. Paul laughed and said he couldn't be more honored.

The Exit Interview

Leon had been working for the Mid-State Hospital Association for several years. His job was to inspect and evaluate local member hospitals to see that they met the standards established by Mid-State. Leon loved his work and planned to stay with his present job indefinitely.

It was an open secret at work that Leon was gay, but no one ever spoke about it to him. As a matter of habit, Leon cooperated with this conspiracy of silence. When the conversation got around to how weekends were spent or what was happening at home, Leon opted out, saying nothing about himself, just listening to other people's lives.

Leon didn't like this, as a matter of fact he resented it, but he felt it was the best course of action since he didn't really know how his co-workers felt about gays because the subject was never discussed.

Where his colleagues' desks were adorned by photos of wives and husbands and children, Leon's desk held only his working papers. He tried not to think about this rejection of his personal life until he began to realize that it was *he* who was doing the rejecting. No one had told him he couldn't have a picture of his lover on his desk. He didn't really *know* that his co-workers would be homophobic. He had just assumed it.

Leon brought a picture of Daniel to work and placed it on

his desk. Several people noticed it and asked who the person was. Leon said it was his life partner.

The sky didn't fall and Leon was not ostracized by his co-workers. It felt good to him to be able to say who Daniel was and little by little he began to talk about *his* weekends and trips with his lover. Still the sky did not fall. Leon was beginning to relax about being openly gay at work.

The day Leon got a call to come to the boss's office he felt the old apprehension return. Maybe he had been too open. Maybe he shouldn't have put Daniel's picture on his desk. Maybe he was going to get fired. It was with some trepidation that Leon approached the boss's door.

The boss was Henry. From the look on Henry's face when Leon entered the room it was clear that this was not going to be a disaster. Leon felt reassured, and when Henry began to talk about considering him for a promotion to regional director Leon felt ecstatic. Henry praised Leon's work and said he was pleased to be able to make this offer. There was just one condition.

If Leon wanted the job he would have to agree that he would not let it be known *in any way* that he was gay. Henry said this was very important, a requirement of the promotion actually, because the board of directors of Mid-State did not want a gay man representing the association in a position of authority.

Leon had a mix of feelings—despair that his worst expectation had come to pass, anger at being presented with such a proposal, and confusion about how to react to it. He posed the question of what difference it could possibly make what his sexual orientation was in the business of inspecting hospitals.

Henry said that as regional director he would have much more visibility and if he went around revealing he was gay he would not get the respect a representative of Mid-State should have. When Henry asked if Leon would agree to this, Leon found that he had no answer. He said he would have to think it over.

Over the next few days Leon struggled with his conscience. He wanted the promotion, he wanted to work for Mid-State, but something inside him had been terribly shaken. He felt sad, then furious that he had been told, essentially, that being gay was an embarrassment and something to be kept hidden. Leon made the decision to quit. It didn't particularly feel like a rational decision but it did feel like he had to do it.

Henry was not happy about Leon's quitting. He said he couldn't understand it. Why would Leon turn down such a good offer just to be able to tell people he was gay. Leon said that, indeed, Henry didn't understand. After trying in vain to change Leon's mind, Henry accepted his resignation. He asked Leon to write up any comments he had as part of his exit interview.

Leon approached this task with relish. He suddenly felt empowered by the opportunity to express his thoughts. He wrote about the lack of freedom he'd felt with his co-workers, how he'd had to be an outsider when they talked about their lives, how he felt good about putting his partner's picture on his desk, and how he had begun to feel more like a part of the team when he could talk about his own personal life.

Leon wrote of his resentment at being labeled as someone who had to be warned not to embarrass the association. Leon unburdened himself of the anger he felt at being treated like a second-class citizen and he suggested that the Mid-State board of directors would benefit from some education about how to appreciate people for who they are.

Leon strongly suggested a training experience for the board and he said he would be glad to help them find an appropriate trainer so they could move themselves into a 1990s mind-set about diversity in the workplace.

When he finished writing, Leon had a triumphant feeling. He had taken a stand and it felt like he had made a personal leap forward. He felt proud of his decision; it was self-affirming and he felt more integrated than he ever had before.

At the Board Meeting

Doug was a vice-president of a large insurance company based in New York City. Having made a name for himself in his own field, he was invited to sit on the board of an important banking institution. Doug particularly liked the opportunities this offered for networking with other executives.

One day after a board meeting Doug was approached by Charles, a senior vice-president of a major credit card company. They chatted for a few minutes, then Charles got to the point.

"Listen, Doug, I am going to do you and your company a big favor. You know we have a lot of demographic information on our clients—where they live, what stores they buy in, what restaurants they frequent, what their recreational activities are. And . . . you *know* what that tells us?"

"What are you getting at, Charles?"

"What I'm getting at is we can provide information on your insured male clients and male applicants for coverage who are undesirable, if you know what I mean?"

Doug stared at Charles. He could not think of one thing to say.

"For heaven's sake, Doug, I mean gay."

Doug could feel his stomach tighten. He said in a steady voice, "Well, that would be interesting."

"Interesting? C'mon, Doug. We could help you identify these high-risk-for-AIDS gays and you could cut your losses by raising their rates or refusing them coverage in the first place. Actually we're doing it already with a few other insurance companies. They are very grateful and we have the satisfaction of doing something about this group of people we all don't like."

Doug wondered what Charles would think if he knew he was talking to a gay man, one concerned about his own HIV status, one who had many friends sick or already lost to AIDS. Doug felt like he wanted to smash Charles in the face. The outrageousness of this offer was matched only by the cruelty of its meaning.

Doug struggled to compose himself. He responded by saying, "Well, that's a real generous offer, Charles. Let me think about it and I'll get back to you."

On the way home, Doug ran through a dozen fantasies in his mind about what he would like to do to, with, and about Charles. But he knew he would act on none of them because his own career would be at stake. He felt the burden of being in the closet as he rarely had before.

The next day Doug found that he couldn't get Charles out of his mind. He was preoccupied with his anger and he knew that he had to do something. He didn't know what, yet, but he did know that he would be unable to focus on his work properly until he thought of something to do. It took several days of obsessing about one option or another. Finally, Doug decided on a plan of action.

Being very careful to disguise his source and remain anonymous, Doug wrote a series of letters—to the Federal Trade Commission, several gay public-interest law firms, and to the gay and straight media. He told of the credit card company's unofficial policy regarding the passing on of information about their gay male clients to insurance companies.

The upshot of Doug's anonymous letter-writing campaign was very gratifying. A flurry of activity followed. There were stories in the press, an investigation by federal authorities, and protest demonstrations by gay and lesbian direct-action groups. Doug was excited by what was happening and he regretted that he had to deal with all this in such an arm's-length way. He began to think about the possibilities for being more open, but the thought scared him. He knew he was getting ready to do that, however.

The eventual outcome of Doug's wake-up call was a public stance taken by the credit card company in support of the efforts of the gay and lesbian and AIDS communities to fight the epidemic. They would contribute to that effort in any way they could, and they did. They also encouraged others in the corporate world to do the same. Many have.

These are a few different ways of responding to bigotry—success stories, alternative approaches, quiet victories—but in all of these situations the gay or lesbian person did not give up his or her dignity or lose perspective on what he or she had to do. No matter which approach we take in countering antigay discrimination, the important thing is to exercise our choice to fight back.

Finally, a story from my own life, one that depicts in a kind of absurd way how prevalent homophobia is, and in a kind of transcendent way how we do prevail against it. The year was 1980. Rand Schrader, an openly gay man, had just been appointed to the bench of the Los Angeles Municipal Court. He was making history as the second openly gay judge in the United States.

Randy and I were close friends. I attended his "investiture of robe of office" ceremony, at which he and nine other newly appointed judges were sworn in by the chief justice of the California Supreme Court. When the actual "enrobing" took place the robe was held and placed around the judge's shoulders by a person significant to him or her—a wife, a husband, a parent.

As Randy's turn came the announcement was made that the investiture would be made by his companion, Dr. Rex Reece. From behind me I heard a sharp intake of breath, followed by, "Oh my God, he's a *faigele!*"

I turned around to see two elderly Jewish women staring at me. Fixing them with the most withering look I could summon, I hissed, "A *shonda!*" (Shame on you!)

I turned back to the ceremony, feeling four eyes piercing the back of my neck.

Randy Schrader spent many productive years on the municipal court bench. He became an important leader of his gay and lesbian community, and a prominent player in the civic life of Los Angeles. To honor him, after he died in 1993, the city renamed a street after him, which is pretty extraordinary.

I like to think of those two ladies who sat behind me at the enrobing, at some point happening onto Schrader Boulevard and somehow finding out that it was named after the *faigele* judge. Imagine their surprise.

"What a *shonda!*"

8

Guidelines for Encounters with Family, Friends, and Co-workers

For many years of my adult life I was associated with a man who had originally been my teacher, then became my boss and my mentor. He shaped my professional values, my choices about the work I did, and the style with which I approached the challenges of life. I loved him. I saw his faults but I was much more taken with his attractiveness and his interest in me.

I was, at the time, avowedly heterosexual, or so I thought. My social life was intricately tied into the social whirl of a high-powered academic community—a dozen Nobel Prize winners, distinguished scholars, and visiting fellows who were the leading names in their fields.

I was a research associate at a prestigious research institute with adequate standing to be admitted to this elite circle. I was also young and husband-hunting, and I loved the constant round of parties that went on in this community.

About nine years into all of this, I came to a crisis point in my life. Fortieth birthdays will do that to you. I could no longer put off what I had known deep down for a very long time. I realized I was living a charade, a sham existence, denying a basic truth about myself. I was homosexual; I could no longer hide it from myself, though I wanted to. I knew I had to do something about it.

Needless to say, it was not an easy transition. I left my wonderful job, moved to another city, and began searching for a new identity. Gradually I found myself, and a woman to love, and involvement with the burgeoning gay rights movement, and a new career built around working as a therapist with gay and lesbian people.

I edited a book, *Positively Gay*, that contained accurate information about, and guidance for, the lives of gays and lesbians. The first thing I thought of as the book was about to go to publication was my mentor, a behavioral scientist with a recognizable name who might write a blurb. Of course I also wanted him to know about the book and be proud of me.

Galleys were sent. I had no doubt he would respond with a quote. I was so wrong. I received a letter from him that I could not comprehend at first. What had I missed? We had never discussed homosexuality, my own or anyone else's. I was clueless about how he felt. I read what he wrote with astonishment.

His letter said that he'd read the book but he couldn't endorse it.

"The fundamental problem for me is the difference between gay rights and gay pride. I think I'm for the former and against the latter. . . . I get derailed on the idea of 'glorifying' gayness, or even approving it. . . ."

He objected to the use, for consciousness-raising purposes, of lists of eminent people who were gay.

"It would be similarly impressive to list great people who practiced incest or sadism, or who believed in slavery, or that the world was flat. . . . What sexual taboos do you believe in? . . . What about sex between teachers and students, doctors and patients, parents and children? . . ."

I couldn't believe that he didn't get it. He thought being gay was just about sex?

His final words were, "It is a dilemma, a predicament. It has no solution."

Deeply hurt, and angry, I wrote back that I was shocked at his equating my orientation to loving another human being with sadism, incest, and slavery.

> Your shallow thinking about "justifying homosexuality" and "glorifying gayness" is worthy of a fundamentalist, antilife mentality, not of a supposedly enlightened, sophisticated humanistic psychologist and teacher. . . . I suggest you start with the terror of your own homosexual feelings that comes clearly through the thinly veiled hysteria of your comments. . . . Until I hear something to indicate that your homophobic white liberalism has been replaced with a real appreciation of what being gay is all about I shall consider it my responsibility to caution gay people struggling toward self-acceptance and self-esteem to steer clear of you.

Except for a brief note thanking me for "your penetrating insights into my personality," that is the last I ever heard from this man who had played such an important role in my life.

One of the most painful experiences any gay or lesbian person is likely to have is confronting the homophobia of people you love, who are part of your family, or of your everyday life. Nobody wants to live or work in an environment that is hostile to such a centrally important aspect of who you are. The hostility may be subtle and sugarcoated, or it may be blatant and meant to wound. In either case it hurts.

Confused and impotent is the way many of us feel when people we love seem to care more about their prejudices than they do about us. Being immobilized adds insult to injury because we are not only being criticized or punished, we are probably reinforcing the impression that they are right about our flawed being if we cannot even get it together to counter the untruths and misperceptions about who and what we are. That is why it is so important to try to struggle with the impotence, to let the anger we feel fuel the ability to stand up for ourselves, to protest being treated as if we deserved contempt rather than love and understanding.

In this chapter and the next, emphasis is on the kind of direct encounters with homophobia that could occur in any gay or lesbian person's life—encounters with family, friends, and co-workers, acquaintances and strangers. The vignettes are offered as indications of the *direction* such encounters might take. They are not meant to be scripted responses followed verbatim.

While these situations may not relate to your own, I am asking you to imagine yourself in these encounters in order to try on the kinds of responses provided here.

Confronting a Father's Estrangement

You have not seen your father in several years, not since you disclosed to him and your mother that you are gay. Your mother accepts you and has been in regular contact with you, but your father has made it clear that he has nothing to say to his son.

Now your grandmother has died and you have traveled to the city your family lives in for the funeral. Your father has been polite to you, but has been unavailable for conversation. You decide that you have had enough of this, and when everyone has left, after the reception, you confront him and request that the two of you talk.

You tell him that you feel bad about the way it is between you, that you understand he is having a hard time accepting that you're gay but that you are still his son and he owes you at least a conversation.

Your father stands at the window staring out, not looking at you. It would be easier for you to back out at this point, but you are determined you are going to have this talk.

"Don't I get *some* response?"

Your father turns and you see that his face is set in pain.

"All right, I'll give you a response. Didn't we do everything for you? Why would you do this to us? You know how I feel about homosexuals. The thought that my own son has chosen this perverted lifestyle is . . . unbearable!"

You feel the frustration rising in you but you are going to deal with this.

"Okay. Let's take this one thing at a time. First, I didn't *choose* to be gay. I just am and I have been for as long as I can remember, though at first it was just a feeling of being different. I didn't do it to you and I didn't do it to me. There is nothing perverted about my life; I am a natural man doing what is normal for me."

Your father looks down at his hands. You are at a loss to know what he is thinking, but you press on. You suggest a discussion of his attitude toward homosexuals. You'd like to know where his negative feelings come from. Since it is unlikely he actually knows anyone gay, you speculate that his feelings are a function of his prejudices.

Your father looks at you with great intensity, and says that what you call his "prejudice" is the way most people in America feel about homosexuals. He asks if that makes most people in America prejudiced.

"Yes, a lot of people are because they have never had a reason to question the stereotypes that reinforce prejudice. You have a reason. I hope the fact that I'm your son and I love you is enough for you to take a look at whatever there is about homosexuality that upsets you so much. That's where the problem is, not with my being gay but with your prejudice about it."

Your father says that you've changed, that you are no longer the son he knew. You tell him that you are exactly the same person you always were. It is he who has changed from the loving father you used to know to someone who cares more about his prejudice than he cares about his son. You tell him that you are angry about this, and hurt by how easily he has withdrawn his love.

He tells you it *wasn't* easy and you suggest that it isn't too late to try to understand each other better, to recapture some of that love, to have a relationship again if he will just let you be who you are.

What Were the Points Made Here?

1. You took the initiative to speak to your father, even though his behavior toward you has made you feel hurt and intimidated.
2. You clarified that being gay is not a choice, that it's not something you did to him, that it is a natural and normal way for you to be.
3. You shifted the focus from whether it's okay to be gay to whether it's okay to be so prejudiced against it.
4. You identified his homophobia as the real problem and pointed out that you are the same person you always were, it is he who has changed.
5. You offered an olive branch and the opportunity to stop being adversaries and resume a loving relationship.

Setting Aunt Judith Straight

And then there are those well-meaning Aunt Judiths, who truly believe your soul is headed for hell if you continue your sinful way of life. Aunt Judith makes it difficult to ignore her since it is her *mission* to moralize you into coming to your senses. She makes it clear that she disapproves of your lesbian life and wants you to know it.

The occasion is a dinner at your parents' home. Your mother and father have worked their way into acceptance of your being a lesbian, and they are aware that Aunt Judith, who is devoutly religious, has a problem with it. You sit through a dinner in which Aunt Judith refers repeatedly to items in the news involving gay or lesbian people. Her references are all accompanied by expressions of pity for these poor souls who are so afflicted. Her patronizing attitude has finally gotten under your skin. It isn't your style to be confrontational but you have just had enough. You wait until dinner is over and then you tell Aunt Judith you would like to talk to her privately. She reluctantly agrees.

"Aunt Judith, I'm glad to see you though I'm not so sure how glad you are to see me."

Aunt Judith sits very straight in her chair, hands crossed in her lap.

"I don't know what you mean, dear."

You pause, wondering if this is going to be harder than you thought it would be, but you've opened the door and feel as if you can't stop here, though a part of you would like to.

"My mother tells me that you have some strong feelings about me being a lesbian."

At the mention of the L word, Aunt Judith's back stiffens.

"I won't lie to you. You know I am a very religious person and my religion considers homosexuality to be an abomination of God. I don't know how you can possibly still call yourself a Christian when you are breaking God's law with the way you live."

You thank Aunt Judith for being honest with you. But you tell her that you and she seem to have two different Gods, yours being loving and affirming, hers being judgmental and punishing. You tell her that you consider your sexuality to be a gift from God, that it has enabled you to be more spiritual than ever because you are free to love and be loved in the way that is natural for you.

Aunt Judith looks horrified. "You obviously haven't read your Bible lately, my dear. I think you are deluding yourself. The Bible is the word of God, and the Bible clearly states that same-gender sex is perverse and against nature, far from being a *gift* from God."

You have been prepared for this conversation for some time. You remind yourself to be gentle as you explain that condemnation of same-gender sex in the Bible is about the authors' profound ignorance about human sexuality and about loving relationships between same-sex partners. You remind Aunt Judith that the Bible we read today has been edited and translated so many times over the centuries that it now, more than anything, reflects the biased thinking of its many interpreters. You suggest that people use the Bible selectively to back up personal prejudices they already have. Pause.

"Aunt Judith, do you think you might be expressing a personal prejudice against gay and lesbian people?"

Aunt Judith looks away. "I have no such personal prejudice. I am simply expressing my religious beliefs."

"But your religious beliefs do not exist in a vacuum. You're condemning people you don't even know, who have never done anything to you. You're being hurtful to them, and to me. Is that what you want, to hurt me?"

Aunt Judith says, "No, of course not. I want to help you."

"You don't help me by calling my life perverse and unnatural. You could help me by trying to understand who I am rather than condemning a way of life you really know nothing about in reality. Can you try to do that?"

What Were the Points Made Here?

1. In spite of your reluctance to do so, you challenged Aunt Judith and created the opportunity to make these points with her.
2. You called up the reality of the Bible's relevance to contemporary life.
3. You underlined prejudice as the real problem.
4. You confronted Aunt Judith on the harm her religious beliefs/prejudices can do to innocent people, like you.

Coping with an Antigay Co-worker

One setting in which homophobic encounters can be especially troubling involves the situation in which you earn your living. If you don't like what is happening on your job, you can't just pick up and move on, at least most people can't. We spend a significant part of our lives with those who share our workplace. Unfortunately, because there are prejudiced people everywhere, they might be working with you, for you, or over you. There is a lot at stake in the work situation, and decisions about how to handle homophobic encounters often have to be made with job status in mind.

The good news is that more and more business organizations are now recognizing that they have gay and lesbian employees who are valuable to the company and deserve the understanding and sensitivity to their needs that every other employee expects. Gay awareness training programs, gay and lesbian support groups, and more enlightened company policies have eased the lives of many gays in the workplace.

Unfortunately, for large numbers of gay and lesbian people invisibility, silence, and enduring discrimination are still the order of the day. What is needed to change this? It's the same old story. More gay people must come out—make their presence known, ask for the support of management, and speak up when individual co-workers give them trouble.

Challenging homophobia can be an awkward business, but hopefully, to be motivated to action, one need only think of the alternative—living with the anger and frustration of allowing someone else's irrational prejudices to decide how you live your life. Put yourself in this scene.

You recently came out to your boss and the word has gotten around that you are a gay man. Most people appear to be unconcerned by this, but there is one person whose behavior toward you has changed markedly. He is someone you sometimes share projects with and it is becoming apparent that he is now subtly sabotaging your part of every job you work on together.

You want to be sure this is really true so you wait and watch for a while, until you have undeniable evidence of his tampering.

You decide to confront him. You go into his office and close the door. He looks surprised.

"Larry, I need to speak to you about what is happening between us."

"I don't know what you're talking about."

"Yes, you do. You have messed with my accounts on the last three projects we've worked on. I'll be glad to show you the proof I have."

Larry asks sarcastically why he would do such an awful thing.

"You tell me."

"I think your imagination has run away with you."

You proceed to show him the proof you have, and then you ask him if your being gay has anything to do with all this. Larry hesitates. You can see him deciding how to respond.

"Frankly, I think this company would be better off without your kind working here, and with all these new regulations about 'discrimination,' I thought maybe I could give the boss a *real* reason to fire you."

This is not unexpected but you are taken aback by the directness of Larry's comments. You ask him what his problem with gay people is anyway. Larry leans back in his chair and with a snide smile says, "Pretty much the same problem I have with people who molest children, have sex with animals, expose themselves in public—take your pick."

Now your anger is rising. You point out that what he has named are sexual aberrations that have nothing to do with being gay.

"Oh no, they are all forbidden. You'd like to remove all the taboos, wouldn't you? Turn the country into one big orgy. If it feels good, do it! Well, I think that is sickening."

"So sex is sickening?"

"Oh no, normal sex is wonderful, but we have taboos

against perverted sex so we can keep guys like you under control."

You are beginning to get it. "Under control?" You suggest that Larry might want you out of the company so he won't have to have contact with a gay person. You point out that you are the same person you always were, that it's his attitude toward you that has changed, that he seems threatened by *knowing* that you are gay. You inform him that you have no sexual interest in him, so he doesn't have to worry.

Larry is visibly upset now. "Don't try to con me. Everyone knows that you guys are only interested in one thing. You are a liability to this company. I'm just doing the boss a favor."

You're certain now that you understand what Larry is doing.

"Our boss is quite accepting of my being gay. He has no problem with it. Nobody, so far, seems to have a problem with it except you. I don't know what you're fighting, Larry, but your behavior toward me is irrational and if it continues I'm going to report it because *you* are now the liability to this company. Messing with my work is messing with the work of the company. Think about that."

Larry is now furious and orders you out of his office. You are only too glad to go, but you pause in the doorway for one last shot.

"I want you to hear this, Larry. I am not going to let you scapegoat me in order to avoid dealing with your own sexual issues. I know who I am, and what I am, and I'm just fine with it. I'm not going to let your anger and confusion interfere with my ability to do a good job here. I'm putting you on notice. Fight this battle with yourself, not with me."

What Were the Points Made Here?

1. You took the initiative to protect yourself from being sabotaged by Larry and let him know he couldn't succeed with his plan.

2. You didn't let him get away with equating gay with such sexual aberrations as molesting children and bestiality.

3. You confronted the real issue in his not wanting you around.

4. You correctly shifted the focus from your gayness to his problem with it.

It is sometimes easy to pick up on a person's conflicted sexuality as the cause of his or her homophobia. If individuals are not ready to accept your insight into sexual conflict, however, you might get more hostility than you bargained for. If this is the case, a few passing comments are enough.

Don't press the point. Don't elaborate. You will have put the focus where it belongs and hopefully you will have provided something to think about. Most important, you have not allowed yourself to become the victim in this encounter.

A Friend in Denial of His Prejudice

Most of the scenes depicted so far are fairly blatant examples of bigotry in action. What you are likely to encounter more often are those subtler situations that make responding difficult because the other person doesn't intend to be hurtful, or even realize that he or she is being so. Try not to be put off by the ambiguity of someone's statements if you strongly suspect that person is as prejudiced as you think.

Protestations of innocence—"I'm not a prejudiced person; I have nothing against gay people; I'm all for everyone's rights"—should not be taken at face value when coupled with opinions about how gays and lesbians should be less visible for our own good, try to fit in more, and not demand special rights for ourselves. Bigotry should be challenged as often as possible. Trust your intuition about this. Denial is an ineffectual defense . . . unless you cooperate with it. Try on this scene.

You have just returned from a protest rally on the day that the governor in your state has vetoed an antidiscrimination bill that would have protected gays and lesbians in their employment. Your feelings about this as a lesbian were so strong that you did something you've never done before. You went into the streets.

You marched and chanted and it felt very good to be voicing the anger and resentment that you and everyone around you felt at being so devalued by your own governor. The media were there in force and, to your surprise, you found yourself answering the questions of a television reporter.

The day after the rally you get a call from Philip, a nongay friend whom you have known since high school. Philip says that he was quite surprised to see you on television, and even more surprised to hear what you had to say. It is quickly apparent that Philip was not *pleasantly* surprised.

"You know I understand that you're gay and you have some feelings about this business with the governor, but do you really think it's a good idea to be seen marching in the street like that?"

You reply that you think it's a swell idea, that it made you feel incredibly energized to be surrounded by people who felt the same as you and were doing something about it.

Pause.

You guess that Philip is deciding what to do with your statement.

"Aren't you worried about your family and your job?"

"Philip, my family knows I'm a lesbian and so does my boss."

"But you've been discreet about it. You've just given them the information. It's a whole other thing to be on television talking about gay rights. How do you think they'll feel about that?"

"How did you feel about it, Philip?"

"Well, I was a little embarrassed if you want to know the truth."

"So my being gay was okay as long as I didn't talk about it in public?"

"Well, frankly . . . I mean what you do in private is your business, but . . ."

You ask Philip to think about the alternative—hiding, worrying about whom you might be offending by being honest about yourself. You pose the question, "Do I have to censor myself to be acceptable?"

Philip replies that you have to realize most people do think of homosexuality as abnormal, and therefore they don't want to have it shoved in their face.

"So we should just be invisible, right?"

"No, of course not."

"That's what it amounts to, Philip. You think gays should not be seen or heard unless they are blending in, mirroring the image of heterosexuality? Do you know what that really says?"

"What?"

"That you basically reject the reality of gay and lesbian people as natural, normal human beings, and, frankly, that offends *me*."

"Look, I'm only saying that all this militant stuff turns people off."

"So instead *we* should turn ourselves off?"

You are feeling angry now and you confront Philip in a way you never would have before. You tell him that gays have been silent and invisible for too long, that it's time to stop letting bigotry set the agenda, and that maybe it's time for him to look at his prejudice about gay people.

"I'm not prejudiced. I know you're a lesbian and I consider you to be my friend."

"I'm your friend as long as I don't embarrass you by being *publicly* gay. Well, this protest is one of the healthiest things I've ever done. I have come to terms with who I am and it feels good. And I'll probably be protesting again, so I suggest you try coming to terms with your discomfort. Think about it, Philip; what you are suggesting about gays not being visible speaks more of your prejudice than anything."

"I'm not prejudiced. If I was I wouldn't be your friend."

"If you weren't prejudiced you wouldn't be suggesting that I keep the lid on my homosexuality so as not to embarrass you."

What Were the Points Made Here?

1. You defined your pride versus his prejudice.
2. You put the focus on him, forcing him to take some responsibility for his attitude.
3. You pointed out the hostility in his supposedly well-intentioned advice.
4. You provided a perspective on what it means for gays to be silent and invisible.
5. You confronted his contradictions and identified his prejudice as the true motivation for his comments.

Are Some Gays Homophobic?

It shouldn't come as a surprise that some gay and lesbian people are homophobic. We have all been exposed to the same antigay stereotypes and prejudices in this society. Some of us have found antidotes to those toxic ideas about who we are; others have *internalized* society's rejection of homosexuality and made it their own, usually in the service of dealing with a sexual identity they have not yet accepted themselves.

To listen impassively to homophobic remarks from a gay person is to reinforce the notion that such remarks bear truth, and that you are agreeing. Silence speaks loudly in such situations. While it may be hard to do, because telling people what they don't want to hear is never easy, confronting gay homophobia is doing us all a favor. Take the following scene.

You are a single male and you have been fixed up on a blind date with a friend of a friend. You are delighted when your date comes to pick you up because he is handsome, well dressed, and sexy. You go to dinner in a restaurant he suggests. The conversation is light and things are going well. Your date asks if you are planning any trips during the summer. You tell him that your travel agent is putting together a two-week tour of well-known gay resorts.

Your date asks if your travel agent is gay. "Gay as a goose," you tell him, to which he replies that he wouldn't want to use a gay travel agent because gays can be so flaky. You are surprised at this remark, and you tell him that your travel agent is certainly not flaky and it just makes sense to use a gay person to put together a gay tour.

Your date then asks if everyone on the tour will be gay, and when you say yes, he shakes his head and allows how he wouldn't want to spend that much time around a crowd of silly queens posturing and bitching. You tell him that you know most of these people and they are not "silly queens" at all, that a gay tour is a chance to relax and have fun.

Your date says, "Probably plenty of sex, right? Gay men are always so horny."

And you reply that most of the guys you know are coupled, so it's possible there will be some playing around, but not likely.

"Oh come on," your date says, "who are you kidding? You know that gays don't take their relationships seriously and none of them last very long anyway. Most gay guys have no willpower when the flesh is tempted."

You tell him that you know quite a few gay couples who are monogamous, to which he sneers, "Totally untrustworthy! I see partners out on each other all the time. It's a house of cards. Gay men are just too frivolous to settle down and commit to one person for very long."

"And what about you? Is that the way you are?"

"Why fight it?" he answers. "Gay relationships don't work. Might as well just have fun, though frankly, I don't like to spend a lot of time around gay people. There's so much game playing and deviousness. It's so hard to trust anyone gay."

After dinner your date suggests you go dancing. You beg off, saying you have an early appointment in the morning. Actually you are eager to get away from him. You wish you had told him how put off you were by his comments, but you didn't want to get further involved by confronting him. It wasn't quite that easy.

The next day your date calls and asks if you'd like to go out on the weekend. You hesitate, trying to decide whether to be truthful with him. The easy way out would be to say you are already booked, but that is not true, and anyway a part of you is eager to tell him what you think. You take a deep breath.

"I have to be honest with you. The way you talk about gay people really offends me."

He says he doesn't know what you're talking about and asks what he said that would make you feel that way.

"Just think about this; 'Gays are flaky and undependable.' That generalization is not only inaccurate, it unfairly condemns an entire class of people. Then there is your notion that gay men are 'a bunch of silly queens posturing and bitching all the time.' Certainly there are people who do that, but to suggest that this behavior is typical of all gay men is ridiculous, as well as belittling."

Your date is silent on the other end. You go on to tell him his portrayal of gay men as irresponsibly sexual and unable to have a monogamous relationship *sounds* right out of the agenda of the religious right.

He says, "Okay, go on."

"I don't know who your friends are, but many of the men in couples I know care deeply about each other and are very committed to making their monogamous relationships work. Once again, this is a favorite antigay cliché—gay men are too frivolous and promiscuous to sustain ongoing relationships. It's not true. It's damaging to us. Just think about how this sounds, what it means."

"Okay."

"Finally you describe gay people as 'game playing, devious, and untrustworthy.' I'm sure some are, just as some nongay people are. Well, I don't happen to fit that description, nor do most of the gay people I know."

Finally, you tell him that his remarks could be damaging because they not only play into straight homophobia, but into the self-rejection that too many gays already feel.

"When you talk about gay men, do you realize that you are talking about yourself? Do you truly feel that negative about what you are? You know, we have enough detractors outside our community. We don't need our own people putting us down. Will you think about that?"

He says he will.

What Were the Points Made Here?

All too often we hear such comments from gay people and we let them go by. You took the high road and told the truth, and in so doing:

1. You revealed the homophobic nature of his remarks.
2. You were specific in your examples so the person had the opportunity to focus in on your points.
3. You related his remarks to the kinds of statements made by the religious right to illustrate how gay-bashing they were.
4. You correctly pointed out that his putting down of gay men represents a rejection of his own gayness.

Hopefully these few scenarios will give you some ideas for dealing with similar situations that might come up in your own life. There will be varying degrees of culpability in those you encounter. One person may tell an antigay joke but not really be as homophobic as the joke sounds. Another may appear to be accepting but when you listen for the subtext of his/her remarks the homophobia is all too apparent.

Determining a person's motivation in telling a homophobic joke, for instance, may help you decide the best way to approach the situation. Cousin Bertha might be the warmest, most generous person in the world but not understand that making fun of homosexuals is cruel and hurtful.

And while we're on Cousin Bertha, there is the necessity, at times, to think about how expendable such a person might be in your life. If you really don't care if you ever see this individual again, fire away. But if you couldn't think of not having good old Bertha in your life anymore, you may want to mute your anger and frustration and come at her in easy steps, treading gently and with care as you attempt to educate her to a more enlightened attitude.

9

Guidelines for Encounters with Acquaintances and Strangers

"Have you heard the one about the faggot who . . ."

Most of us, at one time, have had to endure being present when an antigay or lesbian joke was told. What do you do?

Do you stand there with a smile frozen on your face? Do you laugh weakly? Do you walk away? Of course, what you would like to do is to confront the joke teller, but for many people the prospect of doing that is just too daunting. You don't know the joke teller well, or at all, you can't predict what you will have to deal with. You opt out, but wouldn't it feel good not to? Try this.

You have been taken to a party by friends. You find yourself standing in a group of strangers, listening to their discussion. There are several men and three other women besides yourself. When there is a lull in the conversation, one of the men says, "Hey, listen to this one," and he proceeds to tell an antigay joke. Everyone laughs, except you. You look around trying to discern if there is anyone else gay in the group. Apparently not.

You want to say something to this guy, but you aren't sure what to say. Also, it feels as if you are in unfriendly territory. The chances of being agreed with, or even heard, seem slim, so why take the chance? But if you don't say something soon the opportunity will be gone.

You take a deep breath, and say, "Excuse me, but I find that joke offensive."

Everyone turns and stares at you. You'd like to disappear into the woodwork, but it's too late for that. The joke teller asks what your problem is with his little story. Another deep breath. You answer that the joke ridicules people unfairly.

The answer you get is, "So? This is not about you. It's about the guys in the light loafers. What does that have to do with you?"

The iron is in the fire. All eyes are on you. You can't chicken out. You take another deep breath.

"I find the joke offensive because it makes fun of gay people and I'm a gay person."

The joke teller rolls his eyes. "Oh come on, I didn't mean anything by it. What's the big deal?"

You are into this now. You tell him that the big deal is that if no one objects to a bigoted joke the message is that bigotry is acceptable.

"Wait a minute, I tell a little joke and now I'm Adolf Hitler?"

You point out that his "little joke" is hostile because it reinforces the kind of false stereotypes about gay people that keeps prejudice alive.

The joke teller laughs and says okay, he will think twice before telling a joke in front of a lesbian again. You are not going to let him get away with that one.

The trouble is you aren't going to know if you're telling your joke in front of a lesbian, or a gay man, or someone who is a mother, or sister, or child of a gay person. Maybe you could think about abandoning your gay jokes because they say more about who *you* are than you may want them to.

What Were the Points Made Here?

You put a whole different face on this man's homophobic joke telling:

1. You took the risk of asserting yourself with these strangers, creating the opportunity for them to hear a different point of view.
2. You did not let him put you off with "this is not about you," and made the point that any joke ridiculing gays is hurtful to every gay person.
3. You explained the importance of objecting to bigoted jokes, that it amounts to objecting to bigotry.
4. You confronted the perception, at least, that he made himself look like a bigot.
5. You alerted him to the fact that any time he tells a hurtful antigay joke a gay person, or someone who loves a gay person, may be listening.

AIDS Education

Sometimes we find ourselves in positions we would not have designed for ourselves. You probably would not volunteer to lecture nongay people about homosexuality, or AIDS, nor would you take it upon yourself to become a spokesperson for the gay and lesbian community. You mind your own business and hope that others will do the same.

Then there are those times when it becomes impossible to ignore something happening right in your face, something that is so distorted, or cruel, or senseless that you have to speak up even though you'd rather not. Put yourself in the scene below.

You have decided to take a trip on an ocean liner because it's something you've never done and it always sounded so romantic. The first night out, at dinner, you meet your tablemates. You are the only single man at the table. There are the Schultzes, a businessman from Pittsburgh and his wife; the Cranes, a retired insurance salesman and his wife; and an unmarried schoolteacher of a certain age, Ms. Caulfield.

The conversation starts out benignly enough—the weather, the accommodations, the various ports of call. Somewhere around dessert Mr. Schultz makes the observation that the two men at the next table look like "you know whats." You look around and sure enough there are a couple of brethren. You wonder why you weren't put at their table, but then no one asked for your sexual orientation when you came onboard.

Mr. Schultz makes the observation that one of the men at the next table looks thin and peaked. "God, I hope we aren't being exposed to AIDS here. Why don't those damn people stay at home? Decent folks shouldn't have to put up with this."

You say nothing but your heart is beating faster than you'd like it to. Mrs. Crane, a dour lady with a grimace permanently creased into her face, says that she thinks these gays got what they deserved and she doesn't feel one bit sorry for them.

Mr. Crane adds, "There are some people in our church . . . their son called them and told them that he had AIDS. They didn't even know he had that lifestyle. He wanted to come home to be taken care of but they told him no, they didn't want to be infected by him and, anyway, what would they tell the neighbors? They asked him to stay away, and I think they were absolutely right."

Ms. Caulfield looks at her hands as she speaks. She says she feels sorry for "those people," that they are victims of their own excesses and they can't help themselves.

Mr. Schultz hardly lets her finish her sentence. "Well, I'm not going to feel sorry for them. They're irresponsible. They've infected half the damn world and we're all at risk now. We're at risk just being on this ship with them. Who knows what they'll leave their germs on!"

Your anger has now reached the level of fury but you feel scared into silence. You have no idea what these people will do if you speak up. Mrs. Crane says in a low voice, "I think we should ask to have our table moved."

That does it, you've kept still long enough. The adrenaline is flowing and you feel as if you have no choice but to speak.

"Excuse me, I don't claim to be an AIDS expert but I do know that the virus is not carried in the air, it dies almost instantly outside the body. It can only be transmitted through certain kinds of sexual activity or by sharing contaminated needles, or receiving an infected blood transfusion. My guess is no one at this table is going to have sex with those fellows or shoot up sharing a needle, or have a blood transfusion during this cruise, so I think we're all perfectly safe."

Five faces are staring at you. Mr. Schultz's eyes have narrowed as he takes your measure.

You explain, "AIDS is caused by a virus, it's not punishment for wrongdoing. No one deserves to get sick and die in their twenties or thirties or at the high point of their life in their forties. No one deserves that."

Mr. Crane responds by asking if they don't deserve it even if they brought it on themselves.

You explain further that when this all started there was no way to know that a deadly virus was being transmitted. There was no protection against it because people didn't know it was there. No one knowingly became infected or infected anyone else.

Mr. Schultz says, "Well, that was a long time ago. Why are all these people getting sick now? They know about your 'deadly virus' now, don't they?"

You go on with AIDS 101 by telling them that the virus has

a long incubation period, ten or twelve years sometimes, and that AIDS education, in the schools and elsewhere, is now making a big difference in how many people get infected.

Mrs. Crane jumps in, "Now that is something that I think is outrageous—'AIDS education,' teaching sex to children. That sort of thing should be kept in the family."

You can't let that one go by. You point out that in most families sex is not talked about at all, and children find out about it on their own, that young people are having sex at the beginning of adolescence whether they're taught about it or not. They do, however, need to be taught about safer sex— about how not to get infected. Teaching that in schools can save lives.

Mr. Crane is becoming agitated. "What you are suggesting is absolutely subversive to family life. We have a right to pass on our own values, not to have that function taken over by the schools. Family values are very important to us."

You take a deep breath and try to say the following in an even voice: "If your idea of family values is to refuse to allow a dying son to come home to spend his last days, then cruelty must be one of the family values you're talking about."

Mr. Crane just glares at you. Mrs. Crane looks into her plate. Ms. Caulfield fixes you with a quizzical look. "Are you one of them?"

You can't get the words out fast enough. "I most certainly am a gay man."

Ms. Caulfield stammers, "I . . . I hope you are okay."

You say you couldn't be better, ignoring what you know she is really asking.

Ms. Caulfield: "Good, so I don't have to worry about you."

Her condescending tone angers you even more. You tell her that she doesn't have to worry about you but she might try worrying about people who are so tangled up in their prejudices they have no compassion for a suffering human being, and that is something for everyone to worry about. With that you excuse yourself from the tablemates from hell.

What Were the Points Made Here?

1. You provided accurate information about the AIDS virus to replace their distorted ideas about it.
2. You countered the homophobic notion that AIDS is punishment for sexual excesses.
3. You confronted their narrow thinking about safe sex education.
4. You put in perspective the danger posed by people so caught up in their bigotry that they became incapable of compassion for any human being who is different from them, even if it might be their own son.

Setting Strangers Straight

The courage to assert moral authority with strangers is not in great supply for most of us. We give in to fear, feel foolish, shy, intimidated. It's often easier to just turn away from conflict. But there are situations we cannot, should not, turn away from no matter how we feel. In homophobic encounters the challenge is to respond, to tell the truth, to set the record straight, as you do in the next scene.

You are on an airplane sitting in a row with two other women. You listen to your two seatmates discuss the article one of them is reading on the growing prominence of gays in America.

Window seat says, "Where have all these gay people come from? Don't you think there are a lot more of them now than there were before?"

Middle seat says that it certainly seems that way since you can't seem to get away from hearing about them lately. She wonders if something is happening to turn people gay that wasn't happening before.

Window seat: "This article says that they are being ordained ministers in some churches. Now you know that's not right. Imagine having a homosexual performing marriages and baptizing babies."

Middle seat says it gives her the shivers to think about it.

Window seat: "And how about this—it says that many lesbians and gay men are becoming parents, having their own children or adopting. Can you imagine a worse thing to do to a child? And, *gay men* having their own children. Now that is where I'd draw the line. You know what those guys will do with those children. I mean it's obvious that's why they want to have children!"

You are about to explode listening to this, but you aren't sure just what to do about it. With each comment you are becoming more agitated. You think how pleasurable it would be to reach across to these women and rip their throats out. You wish you weren't so civilized, and so realistic about what the consequences of that action would be. Words are the only safe weapon, but you feel so angry you can't even think of the words you want to say.

Finally, the last straw.

Window seat: "I think it should be against the law for homosexuals to have children!"

You can no longer sit passively by and listen to this. You just have to say something, but the thought of confronting these women is a little scary. You ask yourself why. What is there to lose? Nothing but your composure probably. What is there to gain? That's a good question. If you speak up you won't have to sit there feeling like a volcano about to erupt.

You instruct yourself to do this calmly, as you say, "Excuse me, I couldn't help but overhear your conversation. I hope you don't mind." (You smile sweetly.)

Your seatmates smile back, but the smile fades as you continue. You tell them that you happen to know a lot about these things they've been discussing because you are gay yourself and you have many gay and lesbian friends who are parents and some who are members of the clergy. You say that you know some of this stuff is puzzling because it is new and you offer to help them with what they might not understand. This earns you a disdainful glance as one of the women looks meaningfully at the other.

You ignore this and press on. "I'm Melinda." You extend your hand and each of the women shakes it limply. You lean forward, eager that not a word of what you are going to say be missed. As you do this the two women push back against their seats trying to get another inch of distance away from you.

Answering a question that hasn't been asked, you offer the idea that there are not more gay people around than there used to be, there are more gay people deciding not to hide who they are, to be open about their lives, to be honest. (Another sweet smile.)

The two women are staring at you now. You are not sure if they are trying to figure out why you are oppressing them in this manner or if they are really listening to you.

On to the next unasked question. You tell them that many religious leaders have accepted gays and lesbians as being able to serve God just as well as people who are not gay. If it's okay with them shouldn't it be okay with all of us?

Both women are now staring at the seat in front of them. Again you aren't sure if they are contemplating your words, or pretending that you don't exist.

You go on to talk about gay and lesbian people as parents, how gays want to give life, to nurture, to love children just like anyone else. You say that the children of gays and lesbians are very much wanted, planned for, and cherished, unlike the children of some nongays. You say that gay men are particularly dedicated and protective fathers who wouldn't allow any harm to their children from anyone.

You respond to their concerns about children of gays being discriminated against by pointing out that ethnic minorities are not told that they shouldn't have children because they might be discriminated against, that all bigotry can be best dealt with by preparing children for it—by loving and valuing them at home so they are strong, resilient human beings.

You know that these women are hearing you even though they pretend not to be. Fine. You have a final statement:

"Now, if there is anything else you're puzzled about I would be glad to help. I know that if you aren't acquainted with gay people you would have no way of knowing the truth about these things."

Neither woman looks up.

"So I'll be right here if you think of something you want to ask or to discuss further."

In spite of the cold shoulder you have received you feel triumphant, as though a burden has been lifted—the burden of bearing in silence the pain of being misunderstood and trivialized.

What Were the Points Made Here?

1. You demonstrated to the women that they can't take it for granted that anyone overhearing such a conversation either agrees with or doesn't care about the homophobia being expressed.
2. You corrected the notion that more people are "turning gay," and explained that gays have always been there, but are coming out more and therefore are more visible.
3. You informed them of the acceptance of many religious leaders to gays and lesbians being clergy.
4. You explained why gay and lesbian people want to become parents and addressed the issue of potential discrimination in perspective.

The Struggle within Yourself

In the above examples you were able to stand up to homophobic people and say what you wanted. Few people in this society find confrontation easy, especially when you must reveal something about yourself in the process that could put you at risk. The conflict is illustrated in this scene.

You've just started a new job working for a family-owned retail business. The head of the family, and of the business, is John. In your contacts with him so far, he has been friendly, pleasant, and helpful. You soon learn that John and his entire family are devout fundamentalist Christians. You have not told John that you are a gay man and on learning of his religious affiliation you decide it is the better part of wisdom not to tell.

One day, a young man comes into the store with an armful of flyers for an AIDS charity event. He asks if he could leave a few on the counter. John becomes furious and orders the young man out of the store. You don't have to ask what John's anger is about. It is all too obvious. You are upset over this, but feel helpless to do anything about it. You try to put it out of your mind but it nags at you.

Several weeks later two men come into the store. From the way they behave toward each other, it is obvious they are lovers. You wait on them, feeling nervous because you can see John watching you from the back of the store. The two men are gregarious types who engage you in conversation, which makes you even more nervous.

You are glad when they leave, and sure enough, here comes John with a sour look on his face. He tells you that he hopes they will be dissatisfied customers so they won't come back because he is repulsed by their kind. He asks if you watched them carefully and are sure they didn't steal anything.

You feel the tips of your ears getting warm. How dare he be so unfair to people he doesn't even know. You want to shout at him that you are "their kind" too, that people are not thieves just because they're gay, that his bigoted attitude is what is repulsive. But, you say nothing. You just mumble, "There was no problem," and walk away.

After that, you think about quitting, but jobs are hard to

find these days. You think about telling John that you are gay. Maybe now that he knows a gay person his attitude might change. And then you realize that it isn't *his* attitude you'd like to change, it's your own.

You get in touch with the anger you feel at having to censor yourself just because you are talking to gay men. You resent John's assumption that you share his bigoted values. You hate having to swallow your feelings when you really want to turn up the volume on them full blast. You are disappointed in yourself for being struck dumb, immobilized, afraid to assert yourself.

And then you realize that it isn't just the job that is keeping you from speaking up. It's the fear, a nameless fear seeded at a young age, that something disastrous will befall you if you challenge authority, demand understanding, create discord. All of it. Any of it. You opt out to be safe. You've been doing it all your life. You're still doing it. You want to stop, but you're not sure you know how to do that.

It seems it should be so simple. You just open your mouth and say what you have to say, and if John doesn't like it you move on. At least you will have freed yourself from his bigotry and from your own fear and inertia. You determine that you will do that soon, very soon.

It is a step in the right direction to get in touch with the feelings and thoughts that underlie our fears. "What am I afraid of?" is a question worth asking when the ability to challenge ignorance and prejudice is inhibited by a sense of powerlessness. It is important to sort out how much of that sense of powerlessness is a function of contemporary reality and how much of it is tied to anxieties built into a forming personality.

"Don't talk back. Mind your manners. Respect your elders. Keep quiet. Don't bother us."

Does all this translate to a fear of confrontation in adult life? It can, and does, for many people. Fear creates a moratorium on courage. The real test is to be able to put your fear in perspective and do what you thought you couldn't do. It doesn't mean you are no longer afraid. It means you are no longer a prisoner of your fear. You have to risk in order to learn what you are capable of. You have to move beyond fear to discover the courage.

10

Going Public—Radio, Television, Other Forums

There are many ways to *go public* in the fight against homophobia. Actually, you are going public when you put a picture of your lover on your desk at work and then answer honestly when asked who that is. You go public every time you disclose to someone that you are gay or lesbian, every time you don't allow the "heterosexual assumption" to identify you as straight.

Going public in these ways is a big step for many people who are just coming to grips with a gay identity. Others, who have been there and done that, will be ready for the kind of steps I describe below, which may sound like giant leaps into the void for those who are moving slowly out of their closet. The pace at which you move should be of your own design, though that can be complicated in this age of activism by those on the sidelines trying to *hurry* you out of the closet.

You will follow your own rhythm in moving toward whatever form of going public you choose. My job is to present some of the opportunities there are to be a part of the action when you decide that you want to do that. These opportunities are around in almost every city. You have only to ferret them out when you are ready.

For example, you might make yourself available to participate in a public forum debating some gay-related issue. You might become part of a speakers' bureau providing diverse groups with accurate information about what it means to be gay or lesbian.

You might be interviewed for a print publication or appear on radio or television as an openly gay person. Or you might just choose to address some affinity group in your life—a class, a club, a group from your congregation, or a gathering in your neighborhood.

As the religious right presses its antigay ballot initiatives in towns and cities across the country, people who never had any reason to talk about homosexuality find themselves pondering the pros and cons of gay rights. *Our* issues are on the table, and the call is out for gay men and lesbians willing to be part of the debate.

Why would *you* become involved? Perhaps you've just had enough of sitting on the sidelines. You've been angered at what you hear from homophobic people. You are impatient with good people who don't understand our side of the story because they have never heard it. Or, you want to be in on the action, taking advantage of the new opportunities to express yourself as a gay or lesbian person, to educate and enlighten rather than stewing silently about injustice and discrimination.

When, if, you make the decision to go public you may have initial fears about the consequences or just about the experience of revealing yourself. If you are like most people your fears will abate and be replaced by a feeling of excitement. Opening up in ways you never have before can be wonderfully freeing.

You feel the potency of being able to send a message that is central to your being: I am natural. I am understandable. My needs are the same as yours. I am real and I will not let you disparage my reality.

If you do make the self-affirming decision to go public, the quality of your experience will be influenced by how well prepared you are. This chapter is particularly designed to help ready you for any form of going public that involves "next steps" such as making a personal appearance, live in front of a group, or on radio or television.

Please don't skip the next few pages if you are certain you will never do any of those things—groups, radio, television. There are points made here that might benefit you in any encounter that involves homophobia, even if it is with your Uncle George in the privacy of your living room.

I said in my Introduction that the seed for this book was planted when I was asked in the Denver talk to advise a young man who was consumed with rage when he heard himself reviled by an antigay bigot on television. My inadequate answer was, "I feel the same way you do."

I told the truth. I'd turned down a dozen requests to appear on television and radio shows, paired with known homophobes, because I feared that I might not be able to manage my anger. I'd decided that others could handle that chore. I was certain that there were plenty of gay and lesbian people around who could go head to head with the bigots and come out on top.

To check out my assumption, I began to pay particular attention to the encounters of gays versus homophobes on television. The homophobes came prepared with their packaged antigay raps, and the gay or lesbian person was too often maneuvered into a defensive position almost from the start. I became increasingly concerned as I watched these television encounters.

How could I help the gay people see that there were options they weren't using, strategies for shifting the agenda they could employ, ways of responding that would put the homophobic person on the defensive. I spent many afternoons and evenings shouting instructions at the television:

"Interrupt him!"

"Don't let her get away with that!"

"Confront his lies!"

"Don't get defensive!"

"Assert yourself!"

"Ask him why he wants to hurt gay people!"

I was still reluctant to step into the arena myself, but I decided that I had to do just that since I have always been most useful to people when my insights come from being where they have been and feeling what they have felt. The opportunity came soon when I was scheduled by my publisher to appear on a series of radio and television shows during the first three months of 1993. All the programs were done on the phone from my home.

These shows became my database, providing information on the range of issues one might expect to face, and on the pitfalls one needed to avoid. It was from these experiences that I developed the issues to think about that I present in this book.

Two main objectives emerged to focus on. The first was to distract and disarm my homophobic opponent by shifting the agenda from anything about gay to anything about discrimination and bigotry. The second was to restructure the image of the gay or lesbian presenter from vulnerable and defensive to tough, assertive, and in control.

While I know most of you may not contemplate ever being on a radio talk show or a television program, I present *my* encounters in these arenas because they are where I learned the most dramatic lessons about how to go public and have it be a growth experience. For all my resistance to doing this in the first place, I have revised my notion of what I am capable of. I can do what I thought I couldn't do. I found that out by giving myself over to these encounters with the nameless, faceless members of the Great American Audience.

The Radio Call-in Talk Show

If there was ever a conduit for the angst of the masses in America, it is the radio call-in talk show. There one finds mostly human beings cornered by life and looking for someone to blame. They call with their righteous indignation, their rage, and their despair. The radio call-in show is their window on the world. The callers are suddenly enfranchised. They can speak their mind and be heard by thousands.

No matter that much of what is said is silly or bizarre—disconcerting reminders of how uninformed and simplistic the thinking of many of our fellow citizens can be. The anger and frustration about life come spilling out and get translated into aggression against any group that seems guilty of something.

Gays and lesbians have traditionally been targets of aggression for those who are frustrated by their own lives. The fact that we are much less accepting of this assignment now only adds fuel to the fire, and it doesn't help that antigay prejudice has been endorsed by some of the highest-ranking officials in our government.

As is usually the case with the radio shows, the initial call from the producer, or the host, is the essence of amiability. You are given the impression that you are going to have a lovely tête-à-tête with your new best friend. That fantasy fades after the first few shows.

One host assured me that our discussion would be fair and objective, but his first comment on introducing the program was, "So who'd want to be positively gay?" (the name of my book) followed by a horse laugh that made it all too clear how *he* felt about it.

Another host, typically friendly in the initial phone call, introduced the program by warning that the topic might be offensive to some listeners, suggesting that it would be all right to switch off if this nasty subject of homosexuality became too disturbing. He later informed his listeners, just in case they hadn't guessed, that he himself found my "lifestyle" repulsive.

In all fairness, and to mitigate this not-so-pretty picture, there were several hosts who asked intelligent questions, allowed time for informative answers, and commented in an enlightened way when the callers were just too uncomprehending.

One host was the only woman in that role, and the other was a man who whispered to me on the phone, *after* the program, "I'm one of you." The majority of hosts, however, shared the confusion and hostility of their callers.

After three weeks of exposure to all this, I began to feel off-center. I felt annoyed all the time at everybody about everything. I just wanted to strike out, but at whom—the invisible callers ranting and raving into the air? I had caught their disease, I was infected with their anger.

I write about this reaction to warn of the psychological impact that encountering so much hostility can have on even the most well adjusted person (which of course I am) who is determined not to personalize the contempt of people who don't even know what they are talking about.

It is the better part of wisdom on the radio call-in shows to give up the expectation that there will be reasoned dialogue (there sometimes may be) with rational people (some will be). It is more realistic to expect abortive comments from people who are inarticulate, and as often as not, hysterical.

One product of their hysteria is that they frequently will not stop talking. Once they get wound up and begin their diatribe it seems to take them over and they want to go on and on. The host should stop them, but that doesn't always happen because the host may agree with them or just may not be good at controlling the traffic. Okay, I got it. Interrupt and talk.

"Wait a minute!" "Hold on!" "Excuse me!" Here's my advice to anyone who is faced with this situation. You are not on the show to listen to this stuff, and the longer it goes on, the less chance you have to speak your piece. If you talk over the tirade the host should get it—this is a cue to do something. If the cue is not taken, keep talking anyway so eventually the host has to interrupt. Then, you should immediately repeat what you had already been saying, which was probably unintelligible with all the noise.

I see that, above all, in doing these programs it is important to keep your perspective. You are usually doing the show in the first place for a reason that is important to you. The problem is that no matter what the *original* reason for your appearance you will have to deal with the same clichéd questions and comments from the kind of callers who smell blood and fall upon their phones the minute they hear the word "gay."

So what can you accomplish no matter how uncooperative the callers are? This is what I've learned.

1. By appearing as an openly gay person you challenge the idea that we gay and lesbian people are ashamed, embarrassed, or diminished by our sexual identity. We have nothing to hide.

2. You have the opportunity to counter common myths about homosexuality with the truth about who gay and lesbian people are, and you do this not just for the caller but for the great unseen audience out there.

3. You are in a position to expose prejudice and discrimination for what they are.

4. By shifting the emphasis from a reactive defensiveness to a proactive challenge, you rework the image of the gay person from vulnerable and victimized to assertive and in control.

One last suggestion for radio call-ins. Usually the host will ask if there is any one last thing you want to say. I like to end with this statement:

"You have heard here a lot of anger toward gay people. If you are gay or lesbian, do not internalize this hostility. Remember two things: First, this is not about you, it's about the prejudices that we will continue to identify and fight.

"Second, don't lose sight of decades of our progress. Remind yourself that you are part of a proud and honorable and vibrant community. Whatever hatred you have heard here today is not about who you are. It's about who *they* are."

Being on Television

In the matter of media appearances, it's important to remember that these encounters are not only opportunities to educate the public, they are, in a real sense, *theater*. You are being a performer. One does not approach a theatrical performance unprepared. One comes to a performance knowing one's lines, rehearsed, and with a good idea of the persona one wants to project. Our homophobic opposition seems to have figured this out. They always come prepared with their scripted antigay dialogue at the ready.

Television offers maximum opportunities for the theater of advocacy if you know what your message is and are ready to project strength and determination in delivering it. I learned that television is not a medium for hesitancy or taking time to formulate the best answer. It is about being prepared with what you want to say, and getting it out briefly and succinctly.

Unlike radio, television affords a wealth of opportunities to communicate nonverbally. You can be commenting on your opponent's antigay rhetoric by shaking your head in disbelief, or simply looking astonished at such distortions of the truth. You can, and should, be part of the action even when you are not speaking, and on television you have the chance to do that, at least when the camera is on you.

It is on television that you are most likely to be booked opposite the professional homophobes who spend significant amounts of time and energy speaking in opposition to the gay "lifestyle" and gay civil rights. These people are usually not only well rehearsed but slick, facile, unrelenting, and imperturbable. They tell lies with a straight face and refute any facts or figures you present, knowing full well that they are provoking you.

It can sometimes be difficult to keep one's cool on television when outrageous antigay statements are being delivered as fact. The Reverend Lou Sheldon typifies this kind of adversary. One need only watch this round-faced, bespectacled little man on television to see the *passion of hatred demonstrated.*

As the torrent of his homophobic rhetoric pours out, his eyes light up, he hardly pauses to breathe, his face is contorted with excitement. It is a cri de coeur. He *needs* to convince you of the destructive agenda being foisted on society by homosexuals. And he does not want to hear what anyone else has to say.

So, how do you deal with a Lou Sheldon? *Interrupt,* or you won't get a word in at all. *Interrupt,* to refute or, at least, drown out his tirade. Ask him why he has made it his life's work to attack homosexuals. Ask him if he understands *his* personal vendetta against gays. Ask him what there is about homosexuality that gets *him* so excited.

I came to see that having ready responses can help you stay focused when your anger starts to rise. You have to remind yourself that people like Lou Sheldon are on a mission of hate. You are not. Being forceful is different from being assaultive. You have the upper hand, really, because you know what you are talking about. He doesn't. His is an emotional tirade and should be regarded as such.

In addition to the visual cues television affords, there is the opportunity to use body language to convey an attitude or to elicit a reaction. For instance, I heard that one gay leader, booked opposite Jesse Helms, had been advised to casually touch Jesse as often as possible—hand on the arm to reinforce a point, hand on the shoulder to convey sincerity. Helms, predictably, became unnerved and distracted.

One thing not to be in homophobic encounters is passive. I like the analogy of the prizefighter—constantly in motion, feigning, shooting a punch, moving in, dancing away. In television appearances with homophobes, the major energy in the encounter should come from you. Sitting forward, gesturing, eyes on your opponent, poised to react, stealing the moment. That is the body language of confrontation.

Challenging hatred and bigotry is not the stuff of polite

conversation. I was disconcerted recently watching a gay person appearing on television opposite a well-known homophobe. As the homophobe mouthed outright lies about gay life, going on about the menace of homosexuality, this lesbian prefaced her responses with, "I must respectfully disagree."

Why was she according this man respect? He certainly wasn't giving her respect as he made statements like, "It is well known that sickness and disease of all kinds go along with being gay. It's a very unhealthy life. I wouldn't wish it on anyone!"

Above all, you must never allow yourself to be demonized, victimized, or caricatured. You must learn to recognize these strategies and be prepared to abort them right away. Interrupt, shift the agenda, focus on the issues of unquestioned prejudices, scapegoating strangers, motivation for being preoccupied with homosexuality. And be relentless about it.

Radio and television appearances are "glamorous," and can be exciting as well as formidable, but they may not be the medium of public advocacy for you. I found that learning to define objectives, identify the issues, and refine my responses made the experience challenging. I got over my nervousness and worries about managing my anger. I actually began to look forward to each show.

We are increasingly hooked in electronically to the world around us—radio, television, interactive on-line services. There is a conversation going on that touches on all our lives. You may find you really want to be heard in this conversation, that you have something to say and it is worth the anxiety of going public to get plugged in and say it. I hope so because I know how personally empowering that has been for me, and would very likely be for you.

A Public Forum

With so much attention being given to gay and lesbian issues these days, opportunities for dealing with discrimination in your own community will be increasing. To be the most effective advocate in a public forum it is best if you can do so as an openly gay or lesbian person. That in itself sends a strong message:

"We are here, we are proud, we are unafraid, and you are going to have to deal with us!"

Try this on: I have put you in the center of the following vignette. This is a public meeting. You are addressing an issue that is under discussion in many places—the acceptability of gay-affirmative books being made available to the young people they were written for.

You are on a community panel examining the appropriateness of the town library circulating for teens such books as *Young, Gay and Proud*; *A Way of Love, A Way of Life: A Young Person's Guide to What It Means to Be Gay*; and *Understanding Sexual Identity: A Book for Gay Teens and Their Friends*.

You are the only openly gay person on the panel, which consists of the library director (ambivalent about all this, maybe about everything), a local minister (moderate), the president of the library board (conservative), a member of the city council (Christian fundamentalist), and the superintendent of schools (liberal but vacillating).

In the audience are parents, teachers, and interested townspeople. The library board president presents the case for excluding these books because making them available would amount to "endorsing the gay lifestyle." The city council member seconds that opinion and adds that it would be tragic to expose young people to such morally corrupt ideas as are in these publications.

The minister suggests that perhaps some panel members are overreacting since young people today are sophisticated and able to deal with sexual issues more comfortably than most of their parents. The library director says that after all libraries exist to make information available, and censorship is a threat to democracy. The superintendent of schools agrees and adds that in a diverse society all points of view have a valid place in debate.

You point out what no one has mentioned so far, that there are gay and lesbian teenagers who are desperate for positive, validating information about who they are, and the community owes it to them to make such information available.

Your statement brings a quick retort from the council member.

"I think we are seeing the 'gay agenda' at work here. No teenager can know that they are gay or lesbian at such a young age. This is the gay community's program to enlarge their ranks by convincing youngsters to be homosexual."

You answer that being gay is not something you can be *talked into*. It is a deeply rooted orientation present from early in life. The only consequence of gay or lesbian teenagers reading gay-positive books is that they will be able to understand themselves more easily, hopefully being enabled to balance out some of the pain and confusion that go with discovering society's hostility to what they are.

The board president asks if we are giving these kids a chance to be normal. If they are being taught that homosexuality is okay, won't they lose the option of being normal if they want to?

The minister responds with, "Who is to say what is 'normal'? For these youngsters homosexual may be normal."

You add, "No, not 'may be,' for kids who are gay homosexuality *is* normal."

The board president insists that we should not decide for people what is good for them, since you may think homosexuality is normal but most people don't.

Council member says, "We have very strict guidelines from our Bible about such things and clearly homosexuality is an abomination against God. We must not endorse homosexuality in our community. I'm not sure we should even tolerate it."

You counter that his use of the Bible to justify discrimination against people he doesn't know, who have never done anything to him, sounds like avoidance of responsibility for his personal hostility toward gays. You suggest that what must not be endorsed or tolerated in the community is irrational prejudice, and that we must care about these young people who need us to provide for them, who deserve just as much attention as their nongay counterparts.

The school superintendent says, a little nervously, "Are we talking about 'political correctness' here?"

Board president responds with a sneer, "I for one will not be railroaded into political correctness."

Library director points out that this isn't just political, that we have an obligation to the community to recognize that we live in a multicultural society, and as a community agency the library has to serve all of the people.

Board president says, "Oh, please, this multiculturalism is getting out of hand. You can't meet the needs of every diverse group in the society. We have to focus here on the moral issue. There are parents in this audience who simply do not want their children exposed to homosexuality. Parents have a right to decide what values their children should learn."

You are quick to step in, pointing out that when intolerance of anyone different is being taught it reinforces bigotry and undermines the ability of people to work together or to help one another. Also, intolerance dehumanizes and punishes those who have done nothing wrong.

School superintendent: "Yes, but you know that bigotry is deeply ingrained in our culture and while we may deplore that we have to be mindful of it."

You are right back at him: "Being 'deeply ingrained' is not an excuse to tolerate bigotry. Quite the opposite. What we should really be talking about here is prejudice and why it exists and what can be done about it."

School superintendent asks what *can* be done about it.

You suggest that there is much to be learned from what *has* already been done about racism, that they are not sitting here debating whether to have books in the library that tell the truth about African-Americans because racism has been exposed for what it is—the irrational hostility of bigotry. That battle has not been won, but there is something to be learned from the progress that has been made.

Your final comment is that they must not be guided by the bigotry of some and the confusion of others, that the important thing is to connect with the needs of these innocent teenagers, because that is the moral, constructive, and responsible thing to do.

No resolution here, but you did function as the only advocate for those who would be most affected by the decision in this matter. You argued the dangers of intolerance, and you kept the focus on the bigotry of the antigay panelists. This kind of advocacy is absolutely essential if we are to have new generations of gay and lesbian young people who grow up prizing their sexual identity rather than trying to hide or eradicate it.

There are other ways to go public that are somewhere between being silent, becoming a media star, or becoming embroiled in school board struggles. For instance, here are just a few examples. You can write a letter to the editor of your local newspaper, or to a magazine, in protest or in support of something gay related that has appeared. You can write an op-ed piece about your own experience as a gay or lesbian person. Most newspapers do print contributions from people who are not journalists or celebrities.

You can host a fund-raising house party for a gay or lesbian or AIDS organization, or a gay or gay-friendly political candidate. You can write or call your legislators with your ideas about how they should proceed on gay-related issues. You can contribute a story to a gay or lesbian newsletter, join a gay alumni group from your university, or start one.

Of course in all of these situations you must represent yourself as an open gay or lesbian person. That is what going public
means. You are stepping up and speaking out with honesty and
pride.

Going public as a gay or lesbian person is not only an act of
courage, it is the ultimate assertion of our ability to strike back
at discrimination, establishing each time we do it that the conspiracy of silence about who we are is over. We are on America's
agenda now. There is no turning back.

11

Dealing with Issues: What Gay Is and Is Not

Most of us are not trained for aggressive debate. When we are faced with antigay bigotry, our internal engine revs up to respond but too often the words don't come out right, or don't come out at all. In an effort to help you find *your* voice in such encounters I offer here some of my own words that have proven successful in enabling me to speak up even when I felt stalled inside by anger or frustration.

Let's say you have now psyched yourself up to deal with whatever antigay bigotry comes your way. You are ready to meet the challenge. But there is one more step to preparing, and that is to work on the specific issues that typically come up in homophobic encounters. This chapter spells out some of those issues and provides the information needed to counter the most common myths.

What Being Gay Is All About

Being gay is about the way a minority of our population expresses love and sexuality. But it's about much more than that. It's about spirit and love and community, and being part of a larger purpose. It's about participating in a burgeoning social movement, and sharing that struggle with millions of gays and lesbians around the world. It's about being able to have an impact on society, and opening up new opportunities for the lives of all gay people everywhere.

There's a lot that's fulfilling about being gay once you move past allowing other people's prejudices to stigmatize you. There is the satisfaction of loving someone deeply in a way that is natural for you, of sharing a life, of being a family. There is the excitement of a vibrant community in the making. There is the challenge of being a person who can make a difference in the world.

There is the fun of gay and lesbian humor and the brilliance of gay creativity in the arts, and in life. There is the building of friendships that become our gay and lesbian families, held together by the closeness one feels for those with a shared sense of purpose, the love that grows among individuals who have *chosen* to care about one another.

Being Gay As a "Lifestyle"

First of all, being gay is not a lifestyle. A lifestyle is a *pattern of conduct* that develops in adulthood and is a product of one's interests and activities. There is an affluent lifestyle, a self-destructive lifestyle, an adventuresome lifestyle, a criminal lifestyle, a charitable lifestyle, an academic lifestyle, to name but a few.

Being gay is not a pattern of conduct, it is a deeply rooted internal orientation that is present from the earliest time in a person's life, probably before birth. Being gay is not about *what you do*, it is about *who you are*.

There are many lifestyles among gay and lesbian people, just as there are many lifestyles among heterosexual people. Refer to my sexual identity or my sexual orientation, but do not trivialize my life by calling it a lifestyle. My *life* is about something much more profound than "a style."

Origins of the Word *Gay*

The French word *gai* was first used in the eighteenth century to describe amorous gentlemen of the period. It eventually crossed the Atlantic and, in the first half of the twentieth century, became the code word used by closeted homosexuals to identify one another. In the 1970s, *gay* was politicized and became the self-descriptive term of choice replacing the more clinical *homosexual*.

How a Person Becomes Gay

Sexual orientation develops very early in the life cycle. We know what some of the influences are, but we don't yet know in what combination they work. One influence is now strongly believed to be a genetic predisposition. Another is what happens in the womb—the effect of hormones on how the prenatal brain is patterned for sexual attraction. In other words, a person is very likely born homosexual.

Why Is Homosexuality Most Likely Biological?

People have been homosexual all through history and in every part of the world. There is no one *pattern of living* that is common to all periods in history and all places in the world;

therefore, there is no one pattern of living that produces homosexuality. What is common to our species is what happens in the womb prior to birth. Sheer logic would point to biology as the basis for sexual orientation since we all *begin* life in the same way.

The Scientific Evidence

For over thirty years scientists have speculated that sexual orientation is rooted in the part of the brain called the hypothalamus because this is where erotic feelings originate. In recent years studies done at UCLA by Roger Gorski and Laura Allen, and at the Salk Institute by Simon Levay, have suggested that not only do men and women have distinctly different brain anatomies, but homosexuals and heterosexuals also show demonstrable differences in the structure of their brains.

The Twin Studies

New studies are earning the attention all the time of researchers and scholars who investigate the origins of sexual orientation. Richard Pillard of Boston University and Michael Bailey of Northwestern University conducted studies demonstrating that 52 percent of identical male twins and 48 percent of identical female twins were both gay. For fraternal twins, who share less a genetic inheritance, 22 percent of the male twins and 16 percent of the female twins were both gay. And with pairs of unrelated (one adopted) siblings, only 10 percent of the males and 6 percent of the females were both gay.

The strong indication is that a predisposition to homosexuality is genetic—it runs in the family. While the search is on for the homosexual gene (or genes), with important work on this being done at the National Institutes of Health, findings are thus far inconclusive.

However, the evidence is accumulating, from the twin studies and the brain studies, that homosexuality is, in some significant way, an inherited, immutable trait—not a choice—not a product of parenting gone wrong—not a reaction to emotional trauma, but a natural variation of human sexuality that is determined prenatally.

The Importance of Gays and Lesbians Being Visible

For hundreds of years homosexuality was the love that dared not speak its name, and the secrecy surrounding gay life contributed to the notion that homosexuality was something to be ashamed of and kept hidden. Since the beginning of the 1970s there has been a steady increase in the willingness of many gay and lesbian people to lead open and visible lives.

This new openness, and the political viability it has made possible, is unsettling to many nongays, as is the extensive coverage we currently inspire in the nation's media. It is more difficult to ignore us now or to dismiss us with belittling stereotypes. Our diversity has been made evident, and our prevalence in families, places of work, and the halls of power has been established.

Gay and lesbian legal victories are front-page news. Television magazine shows take the viewer into the homes of gay and lesbian families. Radio and television talk shows feature gay advocates debating the advocates of bigotry. Gay-themed movies are reviewed in the major dailies. Ready or not, America is hearing, reading, and learning about gay and lesbian people. We have been mainstreamed. There is no escaping us.

But there are also still people who would *like* to escape us, who don't want to know about our lives or even be reminded that we are all around them. A common question in encounters with people like this is:

"Why do you people have to call attention to yourselves so much?"

The answer is some form of the following:

"The more visibility *we* have the better chance *you* have to see that we are people just like you. We live beside you as your neighbors, doctors, teachers, politicians, ministers, truck drivers, lawyers, and police officers. It is easier to condemn a stereotype than a real live human being, so it's important that you see, hear, read about, and talk to us personally."

Hiding and pretending we don't exist means we *agree* that we are undesirable. We can't do that and be healthy, growing human beings. No one can. We must press our case for recognition. We will only be accorded the equal treatment we seek when you *know* that we are here. We have come too far to be silent and invisible again.

And, not incidentally, much of the public attention that is brought to us is generated by the religious right's homophobic rhetoric and ballot initiative campaigns. It is their need to convince the world that we are undesirables that produces the antigay videos, mailers, televangelical condemnations, and media interviews that keep a large portion of the public tuned into the issue of gay and lesbian lives, whether they want to be or not.

Some Common Myths, and the Truth about Being Gay or Lesbian

Myth: Homosexuals Are a Threat to the Family Way of Life

Truth: People are threatened by homosexuals for three main reasons: First, part of the myth is that anyone can become gay, possibly be "recruited" to it. Because being gay is a deeply rooted internal orientation, one does not become gay by being seduced, talked, or coerced into it.

People who cannot cope with their own homoerotic feelings because of society's antagonism toward homosexuality are threatened by gays and lesbians who are doing okay and feel good about themselves. Individuals in doubt about their sexuality often become antigay crusaders as a way of coping with their own conflicted homosexual feelings.

Second, being a "real man" or a "real woman" is a major basis for being validated as a person in this society. The successful lives and relationships of gays and lesbians don't necessarily follow these gender-related guidelines. This challenges the "real man/real woman" validation scheme. Some people feel undermined by this and, consequently, relate to gays with hostility, but the real problem is their own insecurity about how to live a validated life.

Third, change brings the unknown. The increasing acceptance of gay and lesbian people represents significant social change. For some people, having to question long-held beliefs threatens their very sense of reality. Opposing acceptance of gay people is one way to resist unwanted change.

Myth: The Battelle Institute Study Proves That Gays and Lesbians Are Only 1 Percent of the American Population, Not 10 Percent As Kinsey Said

Truth: In April 1993, media coverage was given to a government-funded sex study that claimed only 1 percent of the males surveyed considered themselves exclusively homosexual. This statistic was picked up by the religious right and conservative politicians as meaning that only 1 percent of the American population is gay, refuting the 10 percent Kinsey figure that has been used for decades. Coincidentally (or is it?), far right demagogues have for years been saying that gays are only 1 percent, not 10 percent, of Americans.

The 1 percent figure has been used to attempt to diminish

the legitimacy of gays and lesbians deserving civil rights protections. As Anna Quindlen wrote in the *New York Times* ("The Power of One," April 28, 1993), "Those who want to prove that homosexuality is a 'deviant lifestyle' are anxious to show that the demands are disproportionate to the number of demanders, as though the right to be treated fairly depended on a head count. . . ."

Is there a cutoff number below which it is okay to discriminate against certain people? Only 2.5 million gays? That's not enough to count, so we can deprive them of their civil rights, punish them, or pretend they don't exist?

The Battelle Study is not about how many gay people there are in this country. First, only men were studied. Second, it was a survey of sexual *practices*, not of sexual *orientation*. It was *never* meant to be a survey of the number of gay and lesbian people there are in the United States.

Because homosexuality is still stigmatized, gay men in the closet are *unlikely* to report their sexual history honestly. These subjects were asked for their social security number, place of work, and two references. Nothing anonymous about it.

The Battelle subjects ranged in age from twenty to thirty-nine. They were asked the nature of their sexual activity over the last ten years and whether they considered themselves exclusively homosexual. Many people in their twenties have not yet come to terms with their sexual identity. Even if they are having same-sex experiences they are often not ready to define themselves as exclusively homosexual, and would be unlikely to do so in a survey.

Most gay and lesbian people are still in the closet. That means they are unavailable to surveyors, and even if they could be contacted, would probably not answer the questions honestly. As long as this is the case, it is impossible to determine accurately the size of the gay and lesbian population. It is just a numbers game.

Myth: Gay Pride Parades Are about Half-Naked Men Showing Themselves Off

Truth: The people who march in gay pride parades are as diverse as our community and the rest of the world. There are service organizations, religious groups, parents and friends of gays, doctors, lawyers, dentists, politicians, athletes—the media has typically covered these events selectively, featuring only the most sensational sights.

Where some gay pride marchers are playfully showing off, they are celebrating being freed from a time in their lives when they were constrained by society's rejection of who they were, and by their own self-negation. The exuberance on this day is about the liberation of sensuality. The media need to sensationalize and sensuality draws attention, but it is only part of what gay pride parades are all about.

The reality is that you don't have to be gay to be rambunctious and exhibitionistic. Have a look at what happens during Mardi Gras, and at Shriners' conventions. Witness the heterosexual underground club scene—featuring drugs and sex as open activities. And don't forget the Tailhook Convention, not only aggressively exploiting the women present, but as lewd and lascivious as it gets.

Myth: Gay and Lesbian People Want "Special Rights"

Truth: No, we do not have the same rights under law that heterosexuals do, who can legally marry. We can't. Two people married for ten minutes have more protections and privileges than a same-sex couple who have shared a life for thirty or forty years. That is not equality under the law.

In the workplace, discrimination based on sexual orientation is often not contested because coming out as gay might have worse consequences for an individual's life than losing the job. In reality, this means no equality under the law.

On the streets, and in the courts, justice is often not applied evenly because there are antigay laws, and homophobic police officers and judges. In reality, there is no equal protection under the law.

In cities and states all over this country the religious right pursues a campaign of hate against us with ballot initiatives to deprive us of our constitutional rights. Where is equal protection of the law for us against these extremist assaults on our civil rights?

Gay people simply want the right to be treated fairly in the workplace, in the courts, in housing and public accommodations, in family matters—the same rights everyone else has. There is nothing special about it.

"Special rights" in the rhetoric of the religious right means *no equal rights for gays*.

Myth: Being Gay or Lesbian Is Not Normal

Truth: First, "normal" is relative. What is thought to be normal in one place might be abnormal in another. In parts of the Far East it is considered normal to eat dogs. In the United States, that would be thought of as abnormal and outrageous. Normal is not a fixed standard of behavior that applies everywhere, to everyone, in every period. Normal is relative and standards differ from place to place, time to time.

For a person with a homosexual orientation it is *normal* to be sexually attracted to persons of the same sex and to act on that attraction. To deny that and try to be "like everyone else" would not be normal, it would merely be a misguided attempt to conform to the dominant society.

Myth: Homosexuality Is a Mental Illness

Truth: Promoting the idea that gay and lesbian people are mentally impaired has been one of the main strategies of antigay bigotry. Even though every mental health organization has officially declared that homosexuality is not a pathology, the homophobes among us continue to press the issue.

Let's go to the experts. The American Psychiatric Association removed homosexuality from its official list of mental disorders in 1973. The American Psychological Association in 1975 declared that homosexuality in no way meant a person was psychologically impaired.

Every major mental health association has agreed, and there is an overwhelming amount of published research evidence that says that gay people are just as mentally healthy as nongay people. If there is a disorder here it is the obsessive need some people have to condemn, hate, control, and punish people they know nothing about.

Myth: There Are Cures for Homosexuality

Truth: Since being gay is not a sickness, to talk about a cure is meaningless. My heart goes out to people who are in conflict about their sexuality and do not have access to the kind of help that would enable self-acceptance. Some people who are homosexual are unable to deal with the rejection felt from society, and the consequent self-rejection felt inside. They make a choice to deny their natural sexuality. That is their prerogative.

What I object to is the message that often comes from these people that there are places to go to "get cured." This is an empty promise. Sexual orientation is profound. It does not change.

People who claim they are no longer homosexual have simply shut down a part of their being in the service of feeling more socially acceptable. That might work for some, but sexuality is powerful, it tends to assert itself, and then the individual often feels disillusionment and despair—a failure who couldn't become "normal." That is when the promise of a "cure" has cruel consequences.

Myth: There Are Doctors Who Can Cure Homosexuality

Truth: Yes, there are always a few people who make a name for themselves by claiming to do what the entire mental health establishment says cannot be done. These practitioners see themselves as saviors and encourage a cultlike following of individuals eager to testify to the miracle of "conversion."

There are always some people so desperately affected by their internalized homophobia that they will do anything to kill the pain. These are the individuals who become involved in "conversion programs." "Reparative therapists" have been rebuked by the American Psychological Association, which has referred to what they do as "nothing more than social prejudice garbed in psychological accoutrements."

Myth: Being Homosexual Is a Choice

Truth: Can you imagine making this choice? "I think I'll be gay. I can become a member of an oppressed minority, have restrictions placed on my life, imperil my relationship with my family, be exposed to bigotry, hear myself referred to as sick and perverted, be discriminated against by my religion and my government, be assaulted verbally, psychologically, and physically for merely existing."

What a *choice* to make for my life!

If homosexuality is biologically predetermined and not a personal choice, there are legal and political consequences—it becomes immoral, if not illegal, to discriminate against someone for something that is essentially innate and immutable. The political implications of "not a choice" are substantial.

For instance, the viability of religious right antigay ballot initiatives is influenced by public opinion about whether gays and lesbians have a choice to be homosexual or not. Is being gay defiance of tradition and social standards, or is it part of the inherited hand that nature has dealt each of us?

The likelihood is that it is the latter. It certainly isn't the former. When and if a biological basis for homosexuality is scientifically established, gays and lesbians can more effectively claim the protections of government we need against the hate campaigns of the religious right. In the meantime, we just have to keep telling the truth: I did not choose to be gay. I *discovered* that I was. I will always be gay. I am not going away.

12

Challenging the Messages and the Messengers of Antigay Bigotry

Confronting the Contradiction

I hope you will never let anyone get away with the contradiction that claims they don't hate you, they even love you, it's just your "lifestyle" they find offensive. Here's how I have responded to that with a relative who was assuring me that she had *only* my best interests at heart in rejecting the way I live, but she certainly didn't reject *me*.

"No, you can't get away with that. You say you don't reject me, you love me, but you are hostile to the very thing that identifies me, to my right to love, to create my own family, to gain access to the same privileges you have. How is this hostility supposed to make me feel—appreciated, valued?

"You cannot separate me from my sexual identity. If you reject it you reject me. The question is, why do you have this need to pass judgment on me or my sexuality? How does that benefit you personally? If you love me wouldn't it be better to learn more about who I am and what my life is about?"

On another occasion, I was appalled when a lesbian friend introduced me to her straight sister at a party and afterward said, "She doesn't understand anything about my life, but she loves me, and that's okay."

I thought, "No that is *not* okay. If you were heterosexual like her she would undoubtedly know all about your life. Because you're gay she's not asking and you're not telling. Is she afraid of what she will hear if she asks? Are you afraid of the loss of her love if you tell? The silence about your life is an earsplitting condemnation of it. It is not okay."

I did this in my head, telling myself that at a more appropriate time I would have a heart-to-heart with my friend. I could not ignore the alarm bells that went off inside me at hearing a gay person colluding in her own discrimination.

The Courage to Tell the Truth

What has to be kept in mind is that there is a difference between the professional hatemongers of the religious right and the millions of decent but gullible people who are searching for something to believe in—a way to escape boredom, frustration, and powerlessness. These are the foot soldiers of the religious right's "culture war." They sign the petitions, send in their money, vote as they're told to, and campaign to preserve "traditional values."

These are mainly nice folks who don't even know they have become pawns in a power grab by unscrupulous people who have bypassed the real gifts of religion: learning to love others, justice and fairness, respect for the dignity of all people, kindness for those less fortunate, a sense of connectedness with other human beings.

The Christian Coalition, and the numerous other extremist politico-religious groups promoting an antigay agenda, do not represent mainline Christianity. Their agenda is a corruption of Christian principles, in some instances exploiting so narrow an interpretation of the Bible as to justify advocating the death penalty for "unrepentant homosexuals."

We must confront the *perversions* of religious belief that these people are using to justify behavior that is immoral and often malevolent. The truth is our best weapon against ignorance and fear. The courage to tell the truth is our strength. The ability to survive and the obstinacy to prevail is our genius.

The Messengers

Up to now I have attempted to provide ways to confront the false myths and stereotypes about who gay and lesbian people are and what our lives are about. Now the focus shifts to the methods by which the perpetrators of myths and stereotypes keep prejudice alive.

Whether these people behave toward you with malice or with innocence born of ignorance, they who hold being gay in contempt are asking for it—they may not know it but they are daring you to challenge them. Statements that condemn and vilify are nothing if they are not provocation—a call for rational people to counter the distortions of bigotry with reason. The task here becomes a matter of identifying and confronting the various twists and turns of the truth homophobic people use to defame and denigrate gays and lesbians.

Question: Everyone Has Prejudices; Don't People Have a Right to Their Own Beliefs?

Answer: The problem is that people don't just have prejudices, they act on them, and those actions don't occur in a vacuum. Discriminatory acts, based on prejudice, have a damaging effect on the lives of innocent people—they hurt, they demean, they humiliate, they wound, and sometimes they kill.

Yes, people do have a right to their own thoughts, but they don't have a right to act destructively against others who have never done anything to them. Unexamined prejudices are often the basis for hostile acts against strangers, or even loved ones. We can't legislate thoughts but we can legislate conduct, especially when it harms others.

Question: Why Would You Refer to Someone's Religious Beliefs As Prejudice?

Answer: I don't think we should accept the label *religious* to excuse beliefs that are *designed to hurt* people. Is religion about abusing others? Is that part of the moral game plan—demonize people who are different from you, condemn them and exalt yourself in the name of religious conviction?

Let's be clear about what is happening here. People who unquestioningly accept a belief, based on no personal knowledge, that enables them to condemn an entire class of people whom they can then hate and feel superior to, are fulfilling a personal need to prove to themselves that they are okay because someone else isn't.

The Issue of Sex

One of the most confusing aspects of growing up in this society involves dealing with the mixed messages surrounding sexuality. Sex is glamorized, idealized, and merchandised as the reward for being right and buying right. Sex is used to sell everything from instant coffee to automobiles.

We have sex scandals which we pretend shock us but which we pruriently enjoy. We have books on how to lure a prospect into bed and books on keeping sex alive in marriage. We have obligatory sex scenes not only in the movies but also on television sitcoms and daytime soaps.

Sex is ever present in American life, but with all this exposure young people are still told that sex should be *abstained from*. In most families sex is not discussed at all. The underlying message there is that it is something to keep hidden, not to do, or if you do it, don't talk about it.

Then, one day, the young person is an adult and is supposed to be sexually competent and able to enjoy erotic pleasures without guilt. For some people this faulty transition becomes the basis for sexual problems that endure throughout their adult relationships.

Sex is often an emotionally loaded experience because it is used for purposes other than conceiving children or having pleasure. Sex is used to express deeply felt love, but it is also used to assert control over another person, to prove one's competence, or to express anger; and when withheld, it becomes a weapon to punish a partner.

It is easy to see why there are so many troubling contradictions about sex, and why sexual attitudes reflect the confusion and conflicting demands of a sex-obsessed but sex-phobic society.

Gays have been overidentified with sex since homosexuality is so often, and so inaccurately, defined in terms of sex *acts*. Being gay or lesbian is about a rainbow of deep and compelling life issues. To narrowly define our complex lives as being about what we do in bed is an absurd distortion of reality. It would be just as unreal to define nongay people in terms of what they do in bed.

The people who probably have the most trouble with homosexuality are those who are basically uncomfortable with sexuality of any kind. That is one reason it is so difficult to combat antigay prejudice. It isn't only about gay and lesbian people, it's about what is going on in the prejudiced person's struggle with his or her own sexual self, most often with little or no awareness.

About Gay Men: A History Lesson

To understand gay men and sex, one must look at the history of being male and gay. Before there was today's open gay and lesbian community, sexual encounters were the only way closeted gay men had of making contact. Many gay males, overwhelmed in their adolescence by feeling different, became socially isolated. Being lonely and left out for so long, the discovery that there were others like them—others who could understand and accept them—was enormously important. These opportunities for meeting other men were organized around alcohol and sex. There were no other options, so a pattern was set.

In today's gay world it is very different. There is a multitude of nonsexually oriented situations in which gays can meet, become acquainted, share interests, and form lasting friendships and partnerships. Sex is no longer the only game in town, a fact of no small historical significance.

Sex-Related Myths and the Truth

Myth: Sex Is All-Important in the Lives of Gays and Lesbians

Truth: The lives of the majority of gay and lesbian people are as much involved with sex as the lives of the majority of men and women who are heterosexual. Gay people are defined by many things: loving relationships with our partners, our chosen gay families, our biological families, the work we do for a living, our active involvement in the same kinds of social, recreational, and charitable activities that shape the lives of most nongay men and women.

The people who are obsessed with sex are those who seem able to think only in *sexual* terms about gays and lesbians. We do not identify ourselves in terms of our sex lives. *They* do. We do not appear on television talking about what gays do sexually. They do. We do not present sex as the organizing principle of gay life. They do.

Myth: Gays Are Child Molesters

Truth: First of all, it is a long-established fact that the over-whelming majority (most often quoted 98 percent) of people who sexually abuse children are heterosexual men. According to the National Resource Center on Child Sexual Abuse, over 80 percent of the children who are abused sexually are the victims of someone they know, more often than not a family member. The sexual abuse of children within the heterosexual family is almost epidemic in this country.

Second, talking about the gay person as a predator is a de-humanizing and false stereotype the purpose of which is usually to justify condemning someone different in order to feed one's own sense of self-esteem. Demonizing gays is morally corrupt and it shows a reckless disregard for the truth.

It is disheartening, to say the least, that such myths as this one get supported by respected, mainstream organizations, such as the Boy Scouts of America. Innocence, ignorance, or, just plain bigotry?

Since they consider themselves to be a private organization, not a public agency, the Boy Scouts believe they are exempt from civil rights laws. It is the policy of the BSA to exclude gay men from being scoutmasters. Why? Because they believe gay men are child abusers and, even when they are not molesters, they are undesirable role models for young boys.

In November 1993 a sixty-seven-year-old gay man named David Knapp was informed by the BSA that he could no longer be a scoutmaster because the organization didn't allow gays in that job. Never mind that he had been involved in scouting since 1938. The Boy Scouts had just found out that he was gay.

Fortunately, David Knapp did not just slink away. As a re-sult of his media protest the Greater New Haven, Connecticut, United Way withdrew sixty thousand dollars it had planned to give the local BSA council. Mr. Knapp was resourceful, but the real victims here are the boys involved in an organization that embraces prejudice and discrimination in its public policies.

The Boy Scouts who are gay, and many already know, are deprived of positive role models, left to struggle in silence with the message of contempt for who they are. And for the straight boys, the message is fear gays, or go ahead and humiliate your peers who are gay—you know who they are, they deserve it. You are okay, they aren't.

It is policies like that of the BSA that perpetuate the destructive myth about gays as child molesters and undesirables. We should all try to follow David Knapp's example—fight bigotry with reason and guts. And, political know-how comes in handy. Loss of United Way funding, in this case, sent a message that was hard for the Boy Scouts to ignore.

Myth: Gay Men Are More Sexually Promiscuous Than Anybody

Truth: All kinds of men, and women, are promiscuous in today's society. Therapy groups for sexual addicts are full of heterosexual men and women. Sexual Compulsives Anonymous is alive and well all over this country. Yes, there are men in the vast and diverse gay community who are also preoccupied with sex. That is not a reason to generalize to all gay men. Just because the prisons are full of heterosexual serial rapists I would not say that heterosexuals are obsessed with serial rape.

Males in this society are taught that they need sex, deserve sex, and should go after it. That is not about homosexuality, that is about the social conditioning that applies to men, gay and straight. The media does not cover the places where heterosexual men pursue *their* preoccupation with sex in the same way they cover the annual gay pride parades in which *some* gay men are scantily clad and dancing exuberantly. One does not see the action in heterosexual singles bars, brothels, swinging sex organizations, and bondage clubs portrayed in the media. It is there. It is happening. There is not less sex in the straight community, it is just better hidden.

Myth: Gay and Lesbian People Promote S and M Sex

Truth: S and M has gone mainstream and is certainly not exclusively gay activity. There are numerous S and M clubs around the United States that heterosexual men and women frequent in their quest for a different sexual experience.

New York magazine in November 1994 reported that S and M themes have invaded contemporary music, fashion, and the youth culture, with leather garb and piercings being the image of choice for young people and many adults living in the fast lane. The appeal of dominance and submission, and other power-related games, transcends sexual orientation.

Myth: Gay Men Have As Many As a Thousand Sex Partners

Truth: The assertion that gay men have an outlandish number of sex partners comes from studies done in the 1970s, in the midst of the sexual revolution, heterosexual as well as homosexual. Subjects in those studies were recruited from gay bars and bathhouses, situations *organized* around sexual activity. The gay world of the 1990s is about a community organized around a multitude of interests and objectives, not just sex.

Myth: Gay Men Get More Sexually Transmitted Diseases

Truth: In the Alan Guttmacher Institute study reported in the *New York Times*, April 1, 1993, findings were that one in five Americans is infected with a sexually transmitted disease, teenagers, blacks, and women being disproportionately represented. Not a word is said about gays being more infected than nongays.

Myth: According to the Kinsey Scale Gays and Lesbians Switch Around in Their Sexual Orientation

Truth: The Kinsey scale simply tells what a person's sexual *activity* is at a given time. Because they are *self*-ratings, what is represented is the person's *perception* of what his or her activity means. At one end of the scale is the #0 position, which is "exclusively heterosexual with no homosexual activity." In the middle is the #3 position, which is "equally heterosexual and homosexual activity." At the other end is the #6 position, which is "exclusively homosexual activity."

One's activities do not always accurately reflect true sexual orientation. Someone in conflict about being gay might self-rate #1, which is "predominately heterosexual with only incidental homosexual activity," when he or she is really a #3 or even a #4, "predominantly homosexual but with more than incidental heterosexual activity." These self-ratings enable a person who is conflicted about his or her same-sex activity to redefine it as something more acceptable—"predominantly heterosexual."

The Mixed Messages and Missions of Religion

Religion gives comfort to many by offering interpretation in the spiritual realm for that which is incomprehensible in the secular world: a child's death, natural disasters that destroy life and property, premature loss of the ability to function because of illness. But religion is also used to explain away acts of unjustified aggression such as depriving innocent people of their inherent rights—homosexuality is against God's law, they say, therefore it is okay to legalize discrimination against gays and restrict their civil rights.

The Vatican in 1992 issued a document saying that it was legitimate to discriminate against homosexuals in employment, housing, and the adoption of children. While religion is a promoter of love and compassion in most quarters, it appears to be a school for hate and bigotry in others.

At the United Nations Fourth World Conference on Women, held in Beijing, China, in 1995, all references to *sexual orientation* in the discrimination section of the conference "Platform for Action" were obliterated by the religion-dominated countries of the world, mainly Catholic and Muslim. A delegate from one of those countries, commenting on homosexuality, made the statement, "We know that murder exists, should that make it legal?" (*Los Angeles Times*, September 15, 1995).

In an op-ed piece in the *New York Times* (August 17, 1992), Peter J. Gomes, a minister and professor of Christian morals at Harvard, wrote the following:

> Opposition to gays' civil rights has become one of the most visible symbols of American civic conflict this year, and religion has become the weapon of choice. The army of the discontented, eager for clear villains and simple solutions and ready for a crusade in which political self-interest and social anxiety can be cloaked in morality, has found hatred of homosexuality to be the last respectable prejudice of the century.

Professor Gomes refers to fundamentalists and literalists as the "storm troopers of the religious right," who read Scripture "through the lens of their own prejudices and personal values," cloaking their own views in the authority of the Bible.

How the Bible Is Used to Justify Prejudice

The rhetoric of homophobia is richly laced with biblical quotations. Attacking the accuracy of these quotations or the validity of scriptural interpretation is often seen as blasphemy. Because the Bible is a major weapon of homophobic assault, however, we must forcefully confront its misguided use, no matter how much pious indignation greets the challenge.

Yes Leviticus states that "if a man also lie with mankind as he lieth with a woman, both of them have committed an abomination; they shall surely be put to death."

We have to look at the reasons for this statement. First, it was essential to survival two thousand years ago that Jews "procreate and increase." Theirs was a tiny nation surrounded by enemies. Second, since the Jewish faith does not promise a life after death, immortality for the Jewish person was achieved through having heirs, so making children had a special meaning for the Jewish individuals and for the Jewish state of that period. The Old Testament reflects these conditions.

The instruction to "procreate and increase" has very different implications in today's world. We are in the midst of a population explosion. Children die every day on this planet because there isn't enough food to feed them. The crucial concerns of the Bible's authors two thousand years ago simply do not have the same relevance today.

Most important, however, is the fact that the Bible never discusses *sexual orientation*. Nothing was known of such things in the ancient world. The admonition not to lie with a man as with a woman was only about a sexual *act*, and the warning was directed at heterosexual men who were supposed to save their seed for procreation. It is therefore incorrect to say that the Bible condemns homosexuality since the concept of sexual orientation did not even exist at that time. The word *homosexual* itself did not appear until 1869, when the Hungarian physician Karoly Benkert coined the German word in "Homosexualität," which translated in English to *homosexual*.

Leviticus also states that "For everyone that curseth his father or his mother shall be surely put to death," and "the man that committeth adultery with another man's wife . . . the adulterer and the adulteress shall sure be put to death."

In a civilized society we don't kill adulterers, or children for opposing their parents, and we don't execute people for being homosexual, though in some fundamentalist Middle Eastern societies that barbaric practice is still in effect—justified by religious doctrine.

The Bible is an important *historical* document. It is a wonderful window into the ancient world. But the Bible was written over two thousand years ago, when there was only the most primitive understanding of human nature, when life was brutal and people existed in a survival mode. It is the problems of this two-thousand-year-old society that produced biblical edicts. Using ideas from this ancient culture to tell me that I am not all right in *today's world* is unreasonable, at least; irrational seems more appropriate.

Question: Did Jesus Say That Homosexuality Is a Sin?

Answer: Actually, Jesus never said a single word about homosexuality. He preached love, justice, and mercy, not condemnation and hatred. The historical Jesus would have been deeply chagrined at the hatemongering going on in his name.

In John 10:10 Jesus says, "The thief comes only to steal and kill and destroy; I came that you might have life and might have it abundantly." The "thieves" Jesus referred to were the self-serving, punitive religious leaders of the period. There are still many "thieves" among us today.

Question: Was Homosexuality the Cause of the Destruction of Sodom and Gomorrah?

Answer: A careful reading of the Bible indicates that the sins which destroyed Sodom were the sins of pride and inhospitality. It was only in much later translations that the homophobic interpretation began to surface.

The Bible has been through many translations over the centuries, changing in emphasis according to what was happening in the world at the time. For instance, 150 years ago, the United States clergy, citing the authority of the Bible, declared that slavery was a practice ordained by God since whites were deemed superior to blacks. That interpretation is an obvious example of one that had to change with the times.

Watch Out for the Real Biblical Experts

There is, it should be noted, some danger in getting too embroiled in theological arguments if you don't have expertise in this area. Actually, most people who invoke the Bible are not themselves experts and are only parroting words and phrases with which they have been programmed to reinforce their prejudices.

If you do find yourself up against a real biblical scholar, even one who is using the Bible to assault you, it is probably the better part of wisdom to back off. This would be a good time to "shift the agenda," focusing as much as possible on this individual's personal experience with gays, asking what he/she knows about gay people outside of what the Bible says.

Who the Messengers Are

People who were raised to respect the rights of others, even those who are different, do not become bigots. People whose upbringing may have included harsh discipline, parental neglect, abandonment, or abuse typically grow up full of anger that has no place to go. Bigotry is often an outlet.

If one's experience has been that of not being approved of as a child, he or she will likely not feel self-approval as an adult. "Hate thy neighbor as thyself" might be the words many bigots live by. They are projecting onto a targeted person or group the kind of unacceptability they basically feel about themselves.

Some people who are bigots are simply the product of a family tradition of prejudice mindlessly embraced and never questioned. Untouched by the world around them, they carry on the tradition with conviction; steeped in their own beliefs, they are numb to the events that are reshaping even their own lives.

Discrimination against One's Own—How Internalized Homophobia Can Create Antigay Bigots

This is a true story. I tell it to complete the picture of "who are the messengers?"

A witch-hunt is going on where I live. It is being conducted by an agency of state government. It threatens to close down the only facility around that cares for troubled and homeless gay and lesbian youth. The person supervising the "investigation" is, outrageously, a gay man.

Closeted on the job, this person does not identify with, respect, or care about the fate of these kids who have been thrown out of their family homes, rejected in juvenile institutions, and refused admittance to group homes because they are openly gay.

Does this frightened gay man resent that these kids are open about their sexuality, that they accept something in themselves that he must reject in himself? Does he care that they will have no place to go but the streets or an institution where they will be treated with contempt? How can he sit through "star chamber" proceedings where the caretakers of these gay and lesbian adolescents, who put themselves at risk from bureaucrats like him, are told, "We have substantiated charges against your agency," but when they ask for documentation or sources for the charges, he answers, "We don't have to tell you anything."

The message is that the state is sovereign and *you* have no rights. I'm not making this up. It is actually happening to someone I know. Did I miss something? I thought this was still the United States.

Yes, I missed that gay people who are brave enough to work with gay kids are always at risk from homophobes, straight and gay. I missed that one of the most virulent forms of discrimination—bigotry at its finest—is that in which hatred of self looks into the mirror of sameness and punishes whatever it sees there.

It pains me that people like Mr. Closeted Gay Bureaucrat have to protect themselves by acting against the very thing that defines *them*. It angers me that gay kids who have found a haven might lose it because there are so few to champion them and so many who would betray them. That is the double tragedy of internalized homophobia—the kids *expect* to be rejected, the adult caves in to fear and scapegoats the children. Everyone loses.

I wish I could look into the eyes of this embattled soul who would allow himself to be such a betrayer. I wish I could heal the terror that must motivate him to act so foolishly and destructively. I wish I could name him, but actually, his name is legion. *They* are everywhere, the frightened gay people who feel they must act against any gay entity to prove that *they* are okay.

You may know someone like Mr. CGB. You may have seen this kind of discrimination in action. In the best of all possible worlds you would want to confront this individual and expose his destructive behavior as the strategy it is for dealing with his own conflicted sexuality.

You might be able to force awareness on someone like Mr. CGB, to enable him to see through his own self-deception and understand the damage he is inflicting. You would be doing something heroic if you did that. You would be making life safer for many gay and lesbian people, including the kids and the brave individuals who want to help them. You would be doing yourself proud because you stood up to discrimination. You would know the elation that kind of act can bring you.

In the best of all possible worlds . . . but, alas, we don't live in the best of all possible worlds . . . yet.

Institutionalized Bigotry: The Religious Right, Its Agenda, Its Conspiracy

In the 1980s fundamentalist Christian extremists succeeded to the political leadership of the American far right. They brought with them a vast army of constituents recruited by Pat Robertson and other televangelists through their daily radio and television broadcasts. The far right became the religious right, the old red menace became the new gay menace, and political empire building became the religious right's "godly" mission.

Though they are still a tax-exempt religious organization, Pat Robertson's Christian Coalition conducted "in-pew" voter registration for the 1992 elections and distributed *forty million* voter guides. Robertson has made statements about his tax-exempt religious enterprise such as the following, reported by the *New York Times* (April 25, 1993): "By the end of this decade, if we work and give and organize and train, the Christian Coalition will be the most powerful *political* organization in America."

That says it all. This pseudo-religious operation thinly disguises a radical far right political machine that has manipulated millions of people into believing that their allegiance and their money will save America from the sodomites who would pervert their children and destroy family life.

Because they own a media empire (over eight hundred Christian radio and television stations in the United States) the religious right has the ability to drive home their antigay messages on a daily basis. That alone makes them formidable opponents.

Ralph Reed, executive director of the Christian Coalition, refers to the work of the religious right as "civic participation by people of faith." It is in reality a campaign of hate against the rights of women, gays and lesbians, and anyone else it can target as agents of the social change it interprets as a catastrophic attack on the American way of life.

Pat Robertson, founder of the Christian Coalition, describes what he considered was in store for America if the Equal Rights Amendment was passed: "a feminist agenda ... that would encourage women to leave their husbands, kill their children, practice witchcraft, destroy capitalism and become lesbians." Laughable rhetoric if this man didn't have the ear and the devotion of millions of Christian followers.

Religious Right Code Words

You have heard it all, too many times: "family values," "the gay agenda," "special rights." These words echo in our ears and raise our ire because we know they constitute the rhetoric of antigay bigotry. These are the code words used by the religious right in the service of creating a kind of bumper-sticker condemnation of gay and lesbian people.

How can you respond when these code words become part of the conversation? Here are some of my ideas on what to say when you know what is really being said is, *"Hate gays, fear their motives, control their lives."*

"Family Values"

I understand family values to be such things as loyalty, love, trust, and putting family first. The Christian right's use of the code words "family values" is meant to imply that homosexuals are too sexually promiscuous and socially irresponsible to care about family, and would just as soon see family life disappear.

We "antifamily queers" go to a lot of trouble to have children and form family units. We cherish our chosen gay and lesbian families, and celebrate the values of loyalty, love, trust, and putting family first. Religious right values appear to be organized around exclusion and intolerance.

"Pro-Family"

Pro-family means Christian, heterosexual, and antigay. Homosexuals, according to the radical right, imperil the survival of the family as an institution. This supposedly *justifies* attempting to control the lives of gays. One might ask, "Can you give me one example of how a gay or lesbian person is threatening your family?"

If there is any doubt about the use of this code word, "family," to signal right (them) from wrong (us), one need only summon up the names of some of the major antigay organizations in the United States: the American Family Association, the Family Research Council, Focus on the Family, and the Family Research Institute.

"The Gay Agenda"

The Christian right's version of the "gay agenda" is that we are plotting to take over society and turn everyone into sodomites. This ludicrous assertion demonizes us sufficiently to justify attempting to restrict our constitutional rights and freedoms. The real gay agenda *is to achieve the same rights* that every other law-abiding citizen of this country takes for granted.

"Traditional Values"

This is about fighting change, preserving the status quo, and validating the Christian, heterosexual way of life as the only acceptable way to be. The purpose of this coded term is to encourage enmity toward homosexuals who do indeed challenge the traditions of bigotry and discrimination.

Change is in the wind. Empty phrases such as "traditional values" cannot hold time still. The values of the 1950s do not work in a world with a global economy, a drug-saturated culture, high-tech communications, and a populace better informed about everything than any group of human beings before them.

"Special Rights"

The *claim* is that homosexuals have all the same rights as everyone else and what's really being sought are extraordinary privileges and protections. The *fact* is that gay and lesbian people *can* be denied the right to stay in a hotel, be served in a restaurant or store, rent an apartment ("We are not gay-friendly here"), be hired for a job (no-homosexuals employment policy), or (by court order) bring up their own children. The *point* is that there is no legal recourse if any of these things happen without antidiscrimination laws in place.

The "special rights" argument is used to justify legalizing discrimination and making gays and lesbians *political nonpersons* in an attempt to render us powerless in our struggle for equality.

"Alternative Lifestyle"

This is used as a derogatory term referring to the "immoral, sick, and sinful gay and lesbian way of life." There is no positive value to "alternative" since no legitimate options exist for the religious rightists outside of Christian, heterosexual, legally married, and sex in the missionary position.

"Gays Are Not a True Minority"

This is a blatant effort to turn minority against minority. One of the stars of the religious right says, "Gays are trying to hijack the black civil rights movement!" Never mind that the executive director and the board president of the NAACP spoke at the 1993 Washington march in support of gay and lesbian civil rights, as did Jesse Jackson, or that Coretta Scott King has made a strong plea for acceptance of gays in the military. This is

just another way of trying to convince people that gays are social outlaws and that it's okay to hate us.

Send a Wake-up Call

I think a message such as the following, regarding the religious
right, should be sent whenever possible:

> A dangerous conspiracy threatens the freedom of millions
> of Americans. The campaign of hate being carried on by far
> right religious radicals has implications beyond its main tar-
> get—the gay and lesbian community. All citizens in a free so-
> ciety are at risk from a movement that seeks to promote
> aggression against innocent people, transform hatred into law,
> and stealthily seize control of the mechanisms of government.
> Wake up, America! This pseudo-religious assault on personal
> freedom will affect you, your children, your community, and
> your government if it is not challenged and contained!

13

Referendums on Gays and Lesbians in American Life: The Military Ban, Legal Marriage, Antigay Ballot Initiatives

"What does this have to do with me?"

If you are like most people, the intensity with which you relate to the happenings in the world is determined by how relevant these events are to your own life.

I consider myself to be a compassionate person. I cared about the students in Tiananmen Square. I was thrilled when the Berlin Wall came down. I was horrified at the Oklahoma City bombing. Even though none of these events touched *my* life, I felt connected to the people involved. I saw only television images, but the emotions came through—raw courage, unfettered joy, stark terror.

I could safely sample these feelings in myself, watching those people. The immediate experience was compelling and dramatic. I was glued to the television. But when I turned the set off I was back to the here and now. I could think in the abstract about what the implications of each of those events might be, even for my own life—what bold actions we are sometimes capable of, how good freedom feels, how vulnerable we really are to the madness of others—but, click, then it all faded.

With the click, the mundane boundaries of my real life returned. Dramatic world events were shaded into the darkness of a television screen gone black. This, I believe, is how most of us relate to world events. We are drawn to the drama, perhaps aware of the social significance, but our energy quickly goes back to the demands of our own lives.

A problem arises when it seems, once again, as if what is happening is personally *ir*relevant, only this time it isn't true. We are so accustomed to turning the world off with the television that we are in danger of missing something we really need to pay attention to because it *does* have relevance for us.

When I first tuned in to the gays in the military issue my first thought was, "Why would anyone gay want to *be* in the armed services?" I had spent two and a half years in the Military Hospital Service of the American Red Cross, quartered on army, navy, and air force bases, and I knew firsthand that military living had its disagreeable drawbacks.

It was when I watched the congressional hearings that I woke up. This was not just about gays being in the service; it had turned into a referendum on gays in America. Those congresspeople were holding a national town meeting on whether or not you and I, as gays and lesbians, were okay as people. That was something to pay attention to.

I had similar experiences with the case in Hawaii on legalizing gay and lesbian marriage—I didn't need to get married—and the antigay ballot initiatives in Oregon and Colorado—they would never affect me. How very naive.

Both of these situations have great relevance for my life, and yours, because they too are referendums on whether we are okay enough as people to have equal civil rights and have the choice to enjoy the same privileges of legalized marriage as the other citizens of this country.

All three of these situations are something for all of us to pay attention to. For that reason, I am offering here background and issues related to gays in the military, legalized same-sex marriage, and the antigay ballot initiatives of the religious right. These situations have relevance to the lives of every gay and lesbian person in America.

The Military Ban Controversy

In January 1993, newly elected President Clinton announced that he would lift the ban on gays and lesbians in the U.S. military. You would have thought he'd proposed selling children to pedophiles. Senator Sam Nunn, the then powerful chair of the Senate Armed Services Committee, essentially took over the fate of the proposal and proceeded, in the name of impartial hearings, to wage a campaign that brought homophobia to new heights.

Other senators, notably Robert Dole, Dan Coats, and the ninety-something Strom Thurmond proposed codifying the ban into law to insure that antigay discrimination in the services would never be compromised. General Colin Powell, then chairman of the Joint Chiefs of Staff, issued public warnings of the chaos and devastation that would ensue if gays were to serve openly. The lid was off Pandora's box. It was not a pretty sight.

Encouraged by the antigay media statements of generals and admirals and members of the United States Congress, thousands of Americans dialed up their local radio talk shows to pour out invective against the dangerous homosexuals who were threatening the security of the nation.

Every caller had something to say about gays in the military. Worried mothers didn't want their sons' lives tainted by having to associate with perverts. Active-duty personnel were obsessed with the threat of having to defend themselves against homosexual attack in the showers.

Outraged officers vowed they could not protect open gays from mayhem or murder if the ban was lifted. True believers feared the predicted destruction of the social order if homosexuality was sanctioned by the government. In short order, the gays in the military controversy became a referendum on gays and lesbians in American society.

The final verdict on gays in the military was a shameful surrender to prejudice and discrimination. Gays and lesbians in the service were encouraged by the new regulations to hide their sexual orientation or lie about it. Deception and fabrication were to be the order of the day. The message embedded in this policy was a familiar one, that homosexuality should be hidden—exactly the opposite message gay and lesbian people need to hear.

Here are some of the main questions asked about the issue of gays and lesbians in the U.S. military, with answers that represent the truth.

Question: Why Is It Important That Gays and Lesbians Be Allowed to Be Open in the Military?

Answer: First of all, the military is the largest employer of people in this country. Their employment policies set a standard for government and industry, and the message the present military policy sends is that it's okay to fire, demote, punish, or harass gays and lesbians because that's what *we* do.

Further, the ban implies that gays and lesbians pose a danger to those who live and work with them. This creates a climate of fear and hostility toward gays that *encourages* discrimination, with the potential for violence always present.

Gays have been in our military since Valley Forge, and have served valiantly by the military's own assessment. Obviously, homosexuality is *not* incompatible with military service. There has always been a flourishing gay subculture in our armed forces. What this means is that the military has been adapting all along to something they say they cannot adapt to.

The real issue here is bigotry based on long-held, outdated ideas about who gay people are—ideas that survive because the historically homophobic military has preserved them. Challenging the ban challenges the bigoted ideas on which the ban is predicated.

Question: Isn't It Okay for Gays and Lesbians to Be in the Service and Go Quietly about Their Business?

Answer: The problem is everyone else does *not* go quietly about their business. They *talk* about their lives—husbands, wives, girlfriends, boyfriends, sexual conquests, what they did on the weekend and with whom they did it. Without revealing their sexual orientation, gays and lesbians are sentenced to silence or obliged to lie—which means always being vulnerable to discovery, living in fear of humiliation, discharge, loss of career. That is the price to be paid for essentially doing what everyone else is doing.

The message of "don't tell" is: Be invisible so we can pretend gays and lesbians don't exist. It's too late for that. It is hazardous to our health as individuals and as a community to cooperate with the lunatic fantasy that gay and lesbian people don't exist in the military and everywhere else.

Question: Shouldn't Gays Be Excluded from Military Service for Some of the Same Reasons As People Who Are Too Young, Too Old, Too Fat, Too Short, or Too Drug-Addicted?

Answer: All of these are conditions that affect a person's *ability* to function adequately in the service. Being gay does not affect that ability and this has been demonstrated countless times over the decades. There are many decorated gay servicemen and -women who have served their country valiantly. Their names are on the Vietnam Wall. Their heroic deeds are part of military history.

The comparison of able-bodied gay men and women to people who do not have their full growth, are obese, underage, elderly, drug-addicted, or otherwise truly ineligible to serve, is simply irrational. As is true in any situation where homosexuality is erroneously used to disqualify, this assertion is clearly about antigay prejudice and nothing more.

Question: Are Heterosexual Servicemen Justified in Their Fears of Being Sexually Assaulted by Gays in the Shower?

Answer: The overwhelming theme of servicemen objecting to lifting the ban was fear of being exposed to gay sexuality. Operating on the stereotype that gay and lesbian people cannot control their sexual urges, fears were repeatedly expressed about forced orgies, unwanted seduction, and displays of same-sex affection in all the wrong places. The attention paid to sexual threat was nothing short of obsessive.

Since these heterosexual servicemen are already showering with gay men, without knowing it, what is demonstrated is that gay servicemen have always exercised self-control and discipline in situations of this kind. Gays and lesbians grow up sharing same-sex showers with heterosexuals and learn early in life how to avoid trouble in such situations.

Here's the response you might give to any serviceman who says he is worried about being sexually approached by gay men:

"Actually, you are reacting not to something that has happened but to your fantasy about what might happen. Since you have sexualized your expectations, you are having an *erotic* fantasy. It is you *knowing* that the guy next to you is gay that makes you uncomfortable—even if he doesn't look at you. This centers on you and your fantasy."

Question: Isn't Discrimination against Gays the Same As the Discrimination Blacks Experienced in the Military?

Answer: When the possibility of black servicemen being integrated with whites came up in the 1940s, it wasn't skin color that was objected to, it was behavior—blacks were said to be oversexed and venereal diseased, they were unreliable, unclean, and their unpredictable behavior would disrupt the effectiveness and morale of the military. None of those things turned out to be true. The problem was white racism.

Yes, it's behavior that worries those who object to lifting the ban. It's the false behavioral stereotypes of gays being seductive, sexually capricious, and predatory. Just as the false behavioral stereotypes of blacks in the 1940s did not hold up after integration, the distortions about gays would not hold up if the ban were lifted.

The real issue then was racism. The real issue now is homophobia. The problem is bigotry and it is that more than anything else that threatens good order in the military.

While the comparison is tempting, we must remind ourselves that gays have not been enslaved, lynched, and segregated as African-Americans have, that gays have a choice to hide our minority status, which blacks cannot do. Yes, gays have been beaten and murdered too, but being assaulted by crazed teenagers in the streets is quite different from being bull-whipped, kicked, beaten, and shot *by your own government* that is supposed to protect and serve you.

One has only to watch the superb documentary film *Eyes on the Prize* to get the full impact of the terrifying experience that being black in America has too often been. As gays and lesbians, much of our oppression has been internal, though sometimes fatally so. But we have not had to live with the pervasive racism that still promises the possibility of pain every time a black man encounters a white police officer, or a black family tries to live where only whites have lived before.

The comparison that is appropriate is not with black versus gay and lesbian history and life experience but with the motivations behind racism and homophobia—self-validation through condemning others, the catharsis of hatred, and a target on which to project blame for life's broken promises. It is on these similarities between racism and homophobia that we must make our case for combating bigotry in the armed forces and everywhere else.

Question: Won't There Always Be People in the Military Who Hate Gays?

Answer: We know something about who these gay-haters are. They are typically young people from small towns where they have never personally known anyone gay. What they do know about gay people they've learned from the streets and co-medians' jokes. That's what gays are to them—a joke, so it doesn't matter if they ridicule or beat up a gay person.

The military establishment has a responsibility to educate the ignorance and the bigotry out of these young people because it is *they* who threaten unit cohesion, not gay or lesbian people minding their own business.

Question: Do Gays in the Military Increase the Chances of AIDS Being Transmitted to Heterosexual Members of the Armed Forces?

Answer: No, because new recruits who test HIV positive are barred from the service. Also, the Department of Defense has a vigorous policy of HIV testing annually, more often when forces are to be deployed for battle, and anyone who is HIV positive does not get deployed. You cannot become infected with HIV just from being in contact with someone unless you have un-protected sex with that person, or share his or her needles for drug use.

There is virtually no risk of getting AIDS just because open gays and lesbians are in the service, certainly no risk from les-bians, who are the group at lowest risk for HIV in the population.

Question: Can the Military Change?

Answer: Homophobia *is* institutionalized in the military and it got that way through deliberate antigay propagandiz-ing. Department of Defense Directive 1332.14, section H.1 as-serts: "Homosexuality is incompatible with military service . . . the presence of [homosexuals] adversely affects the ability of the Armed Forces to maintain discipline, good order, and morale. . . ."

Also, in basic training the worst insults drill instructors can throw at recruits are "queer," "faggot," "sissy," and "pervert." These are the words used to kick ass when a recruit is not being macho enough to satisfy a DI. The message is if you aren't shaping up you're no more worthwhile than a low-life queer.

Probably the most damaging antigay propagandizing involved the official military training films of the 1940s that literally warned soldiers and sailors about homosexuals who would try to seduce and "recruit" them into a perverted life. The warning was followed by guidelines for warding off such assaults.

Is it any wonder that the tradition of the military establishment is antigay? The point is that they knew how to teach homophobia, which means they will also know how to teach its remedy. What must not be forgotten is that the problem has never been homosexuality. The problem has been the institutionalized bigotry without which homosexuality would not even be an issue. That is true in the U.S. military just as it is everywhere else.

Legalizing Same-Sex Marriage

Some years ago, my lover and I decided that the vicissitudes of travel could be significantly eased if we belonged to one of those nice clubs the airlines have in larger airports. Since we flew on TWA a lot, an application to their Ambassador's Club seemed appropriate. We had been together for ten years at that time, so of course we applied as a couple.

A few weeks later we received a letter from TWA saying they regretted having to turn us down but only *legally married* couples could have joint membership in the club. We wrote back explaining that the states were united in their prohibition of same-sex marriage, that we were a lesbian couple who owned everything in joint tenancy, were married in every way, but were *prevented* from achieving the impossible—legality.

TWA responded with more regrets. At this point my Italian lover got on the phone and suggested to the unfortunate person on the other end that "higher ups" would probably want to know about this because litigation might be in order, and the issue had all the earmarks of one begging for a public protest.

She said that she was going to forward documents to demonstrate further that we were a legitimate couple and she knew that TWA would come to its senses, just as the Automobile Club of Southern California had after our successful lawsuit to obtain a spousal discount on our car insurance.

Terry sent TWA photocopies of our home trust deed in joint tenancy, and our joint checking accounts. She also sent a newspaper article about the tenth anniversary celebration we'd just had and offered to send a videotape of the local television interview we did following the Auto Club lawsuit.

About two weeks later a lifetime *joint* membership in the TWA Ambassador's Club, with cards in each of our names, arrived in the mail. A triumph, but what a difference a marriage license would have made. What adventures we must indulge in in order to establish a simple fact, that we are quite legitimately conjugally connected—a family.

I wish I could fast-forward to 2096. What will life be like for gay and lesbian people? Will there no longer be a distinction made for sexual orientation? Will all the battles for equal rights be won?

Unfortunately we can't peer into the future, but those who live in 2096 will certainly look back on their past, our present, and make judgments about how we conducted our society. Will it seem outrageous that once gay and lesbian people could not marry, as outrageous as it seems now that once interracial couples could not marry?

We move forward slowly, but we do move. I know that legalizing same-sex marriage is not at the top of every gay person's list of what needs to happen to make our lives better. I also know that there are some in our community who may have little interest at present in committed relationships. And, there are those who regard marriage as a heterosexual institution too confining to fit a free-to-be-creative gay or lesbian relationship into.

To these people I would say two things. First, the backlash anti-gay-marriage legislation, ballot measures, and litigation that *will* show up represent another referendum on the lives of gays and lesbians in this country. To ignore that (even if you do not personally wish to marry) would mean surrendering the opportunity to counter the antigay propaganda that will surely be a feature of the backlash.

Second, because there are many gay people who desire the social and practical advantages that marriage provides, we have some obligation to them. We all have a responsibility to contribute to the quality of life in the communities we are part of. I do not have children but I pay taxes so that other people's children can go to school because I want the society I live in to be as educated and sane as possible. Legalizing gay marriage could bring enough added stability to our community to benefit us all.

The issue of same-sex marriage is on the table now, and no matter what cases are won or lost, it will not go away. Actually, the issue has been around for some time. A few years back Ann Landers invited her readers to let her know if they were for or against same-sex marriage. She received more than fifty-five thousand responses, running nearly two to one against allowing gays and lesbians to legally marry.

In a *Time*/CNN poll conducted in 1989, 69 percent were against gay marriage, but 65 percent thought homosexual couples should be legally allowed to inherit each other's property, and 54 percent thought gay couples should be permitted to receive medical and life insurance benefits from a partner's policies. It's the *sanctification* of the homosexual partnership that seems to bother nongays more than the practical issues involved.

What Is So Important About the Option to Wed?

Why do we care? Why is this matter of legal marriage so important to many of us? Let's say you are asked this question by a nongay friend or relative who read in the newspaper that same-sex marriage for homosexuals might become legal. This person is perplexed. Why is that necessary? You want help to make sense of it.

For starters, you might mention that it jars our sense of reality when the U.S. Census Bureau can count two gay people who have lived in a committed relationship for thirty years as two single unmarried persons. It jars us because the message is that our loving relationships do not count, do not warrant the acknowledgment of our government, and, surreally, do not officially exist.

It is no wonder that we have evolved a tradition of failure in same-sex partnerships, a tradition we must fight against to have fulfilling, enduring life partnerships.

Actually, the Census Bureau is trying to do better. They now have a category called "unmarried partners," but how many gay people are ready to declare the true status of their relationship to a census taker? Until we are prepared in greater numbers to tell the truth about ourselves there will continue to be unreal notions about how many gay and lesbian people there are in this country.

How about this as "one small step" for you to take, and "one great leap" for gay civil rights. When that next census form arrives, if you are in a relationship, answer honestly about the nature of it. When enough people do that the *reality* of who and where we are will come into sharper focus.

What is there about marriage that compels this effort to achieve the *option* to wed? Marriage is still one of the main civil rights that we are denied. It would be the public affirmation and a powerful endorsement of the legitimacy of our partnerships. It would give us equal standing with nongays in an important area of the law.

From a psychological point of view, like most heterosexuals, we too have the need for a home life, for the continuity of companionship that offers deep understanding, security, and intimacy. Gay and lesbian people also have a need to be at the center of another's existence, to be caretakers and to know that there is someone who will take care of us if the need arises. And we too have a need for the stability that enables one to compose a life of meaningful activity from a strong base of family.

Can we do these things without being legally married? We can and have, but there is another side to the story—the array of entitlements that marriage triggers, the financial advantages and the legal bonuses. What are we missing out on?

How about the tangible rewards of coverage under a spouse's health or pension plan, the ability to share in social security benefits, preferential tax treatment, the right to sue in the event of the death of a partner, bereavement leave to grieve the loss of a partner, guaranteed visiting rights if a partner is acutely ill and hospitalized, and the authority to make medical decisions.

There are the economic advantages of spousal discounts and the right to inherit with or without a will. Even with a will families sometimes intervene to block a lover's inheritance. With a marriage license that lover becomes the next of kin, with inheritance rights that supersede the family.

Since a significant percentage of a worker's earnings can be in the form of benefits, married heterosexual employees earn more for doing the same job than gay and lesbian employees frozen out of spousal benefits. Is that fair? Should we care about that?

The Age of the Couple

Another reason there is so much focus on our relationships is that the "age of the couple" has come to the gay and lesbian community. There is a growing grassroots gay and lesbian couples movement. In nearly every major city there are organizations in which same-sex couples meet together to socialize and share their lives, to learn from and provide support for one another's relationships.

There are couples' workshops, couples' therapy groups, couples' newsletters, and books on how to have a gay or lesbian wedding, how to build a relationship, and what to do to keep it working.

It is no surprise, therefore, that there is so much interest now in legalizing gay marriage. At the heart of this movement is the desire to remove one more restriction on our lives and to exercise the fundamental right to benefit legally and socially from a sanctioned union with the person we have chosen to love.

How Did We Get to This Point?

The following is an abbreviated chronology of the events and developments that have brought the story this far.

December 1990—Three same-sex couples from Oahu, Hawaii, apply for and are denied marriage licenses.

May 1991—The three couples file suit against the state of Hawaii for denying them the right to marry a person of the same gender.

September 1991—The suit filed by the three couples is dismissed by the state before it reaches trial. They appeal to the Hawaii Supreme Court.

May 5, 1993—The Hawaii Supreme Court hears the case and rules that the state's refusal to issue marriage licenses to same-sex couples violates the state constitution's guarantee of equal protection. The decision involves discriminating on the basis of sex (generally considered to be a stronger basis for a decision than that of privacy rights).

The case is remanded to a lower court, where the state must show 1) a "compelling reason" to continue to discriminate, and 2) that there is no other way for the compelling state interest to be served than through the denial of marriage licenses.

The case now involves one lesbian couple, Genora Dancel and Nina Baehr, and is, officially, *Baehr v. Lewin*, 852 p.2d 44 (Haw. 1993). It is being handled on our end by the Lambda Legal Defense and Education Fund; co-counsels are Evan Wolfson of Lambda and Daniel R. Foley of Honolulu. Because the case involves a state, not a federal, constitutional question, the Hawaii Supreme Court will have the final word. There can be no appeal to the U.S. Supreme Court.

It is thought likely that the Hawaii state legislature will try to enact a constitutional amendment barring gay marriage, but it is generally agreed this probably will not pass.

February 6, 1994—The debate enlarges. Hawaiian newspapers come out editorially in support of same-sex marriages.

October 1994—The governor of Hawaii appoints a Commission on Sexual Orientation.

The Backlash Begins

February 20, 1995—Fundamentalists place ads in Hawaiian newspapers calling for a constitutional ban on same-sex marriage. Quote: "Do you care if Hawaii becomes known as the Sodom and Gomorrah of the world, a paradise for homosexuals who wish to marry? Do you want to bring God's wrath down on our Hawaiian islands? . . . Who has the right to engage in abnormal sexual relations, and then ask all society to bless and protect it?"

March 2, 1995—The Utah legislature passes H.B. 366 to ban recognition of same-sex marriage regardless of where the marriages are performed, such as Denmark, the Netherlands, Norway, Sweden, *or* Hawaii. The Gay and Lesbian Utah Democrats, in protest, begin "Olympics Out of Utah," a campaign to keep the 2002 Winter Olympics out of their state.

March 1995—A bill dies in the South Dakota legislature that would have banned gay marriages in the state of South Dakota. Gay and lesbian activists fought hard against it.

March 1995—A bill is introduced in the Alaska legislature to prohibit same-sex marriage in that state.

The final ruling of the Hawaii courts is expected in mid-1997, and if marriage licenses are to be issued to gay and lesbian couples, it will be following that ruling.

Whether we choose for it to be or not, this will be a watershed issue for gay rights. It will be fought in the state legislatures and in the courts. Already organizations and task forces are forming to fight the backlash.

The Lambda Legal Defense and Education Fund has taken the lead in developing a network of attorneys and law students to research the legal arguments available to oppose proposed legislation and lawsuits on a state-by-state basis. They also plan to develop materials for the drafting of legislation on equal marriage rights, and to educate judges through conferences, law review articles, and trainings.

What can you do about all this? For starters you can be aware of what is happening, and incidentally, the Internet is a treasure trove of information on this subject. You can inform yourself and initiate conversations about this topic among friends and family. It is important always for gay and lesbian people to be out there countering the misinformation about us put out by the religious right.

You can be supportive of the people who believe this is a crucial issue and are working to bring about a positive outcome. Whether or not you are convinced that this really is the landmark fight that others think it is, you can at least be prepared to respond to the queries of people who are not necessarily homophobic but just don't get it. They need accurate information about our lives. Without it they are stuck with the same unquestioned prejudices and we are stuck with the same distortions and discrimination.

The Antigay Ballot Initiatives

If someone asked you if it would be okay to put a measure on the next election ballot inviting voters to decide if you should have the same civil rights as other citizens of this country, what would you say?

"Are you crazy?" would be a good answer.

Well, they didn't ask you or me, they just went ahead and did it; in state after state, and city after city, they have put the civil rights of gay and lesbian citizens to a public vote. As outrageous as that seems, it is happening all over the United States, sometimes with success, sometimes failing.

These ballot measures are initiated, supported, and usually financed by the Christian Coalition and its offshoots. The cast of characters is familiar—the same religious right demagogues show up anywhere that the heat is on to legitimize antigay bigotry. This campaign began in earnest in 1992 with Ballot Measure Nine in Oregon and Amendment Two in Colorado. I think it is important to have some background. The Colorado initiative read as follows:

> Neither the state of Colorado, through any of its branches or departments, nor any of its agencies, political sub-divisions, municipalities or school districts, shall enact, adopt or enforce any statute, regulation, ordinance or policy whereby homosexual, lesbian or bisexual orientation, conduct, practices or relationships shall constitute or otherwise be the basis of, or entitle any person or class of persons to have, any claim of minority status, quota preferences, protected status or claim of discrimination.

On November 9, 1992, 53 percent of Colorado's voters approved the amendment. In Oregon, Ballot Measure Nine covered much more territory than the Colorado initiative, calling for the state constitution to be amended to classify homosexuality as "abnormal, wrong, unnatural and perverse," *and* to bar

the state from passing any law protecting citizens on the basis
of sexual orientation.

In addition, the Oregon voters were asked to approve edu-
cators being required to set curriculum standards equating homosexuality with pedophilia, sadism and masochism as
behavior "to be discouraged and avoided." Also, all existing gay
rights measures were to be repealed.

The Oregon initiative was defeated, but emboldened by
the Colorado victory ten states and nearly twenty municipali-
ties around the country moved forward with antigay ballot
measures in 1993. Some were aimed at repealing existing gay
rights ordinances and statutes, others at barring state and local
governments from passing any laws protecting the rights of gay
and lesbian citizens.

In eight states the initiatives failed to get enough signa-
tures or were successfully turned back in the courts. In two they
were defeated, but this is a Pyrrhic victory because just putting
forth the effort gave the religious right a public forum for their
antigay propaganda. And they will be back.

In December 1994, after an eight-day trial, a state judge in
Colorado ruled that Amendment Two was in violation of the
United States Constitution's guarantee of equal protection un-
der the law. The case subsequently moved on to the U.S.
Supreme Court, where at this writing, a ruling is expected soon.

As the Christian Coalition musters its troops for the next
round of political gay-bashing, various gay and lesbian organizations are also preparing to meet the challenge. State-by-state
research is in process to uncover the vulnerabilities of each proposed initiative.

I believe that here, as much as anywhere, a strategy of shifting the agenda is in order. The issue to be brought into focus is
discrimination—the fact that these ballot initiatives are the
product of blatant bigotry being exploited by the religious right
to turn America into a theocracy with control in the hands of
Christian right political power brokers like Ralph Reed and Pat
Robertson.

When proponents of the religious right talk about the demise of the nation if Christian America doesn't take over (as they did say on the September 1995 CBS Reports: "Faith and Politics") they sound bizarre. Are they not in touch with the *reality* of America's diversity? Do they not know that the richness of a democracy is in the variety of its many voices coming together?

But rationality is not what this is about. It is not the first time religious propagandists have used an impending apocalyptic disaster as the hook to recruit those whose fears about life make them available to fearmongers. Transparent though their appeal may be, ludicrous as it may sound, the religious right has a tap into the hearts and minds of millions of people.

Now, where do *you* come into all this? If you live in a place where there have been no antigay ballot measures to worry about you may feel removed from the issue. The likelihood is, however, that eventually this road show *will* come to your city or state, and when the language of the ballot initiative says things like "abnormal, wrong, unnatural, and perverse" they are referring to *your* life. The person being equated with a pedophile, or sadist or masochist, is *you.*

The prohibition on gay rights ordinances and statutes will be a prohibition of *your* right to redress if you are fired from a job for being gay, or become the victim of an antigay hate crime. *You* would not be allowed to engage in any activity that would present being homosexual as being normal. *You* would have no official protection from anyone's bigotry. Discrimination against *you* as a gay or lesbian person would have been made legal.

Your silence and invisibility are their reward. And in many places gay people have cooperated with that—kept quiet, didn't fight back. If ever there was a time for grassroots participation in something it is when an antigay ballot initiative campaign comes to where you live.

What can you do? You can begin with the people closest to you, telling them what the ballot measure that has come to your state or city can mean for *your* life. You can write letters educating local community leaders and clergy. You can write to your representatives in government, call their offices to go on record with your point of view.

You can stuff envelopes for a local gay organization, be part of a telephone bank, walk the precincts, speak to community groups, register voters, and, when the election comes up, get out those voters whom you have reason to believe will be on your side.

Apathy is public enemy number one, especially in off-year elections, when many of these initiatives crop up. When it comes to the bottom line in elections, it's the numbers that count. The religious right knows where to find its people, how to educate them, what to do to get them to the polls. The gay and lesbian community has got to begin doing the same. We have to get to the nonpolitical gays and to the nongays who think this issue has nothing to do with them.

We have to convince people that bigotry and discrimination cast a long shadow over everyone's life, that they would not like it either if their well-being was being put to a public vote. Most people would not stand for that. You should not stand for it either, and your relatives and friends and co-workers shouldn't stand for it. Whether they do or not will be up to you.

14

Final Words: The Good News

The Holocaust never happened, blacks are constitutionally inferior to whites, gays are sexual predators. If these ideas did not have such deadly serious consequences they would be farcical. It is the way of extremists to concoct bizarre lies to justify their flawed ideologies. While many can see through these mythic distortions, there are those who will not. This is the trickle-down effect of extremist ideas to nonextremist people who then, unthinkingly, integrate such fictions into their own beliefs.

For instance, the majority of decent Americans believe that gays and lesbians should not be discriminated against, but they also believe that we should not be allowed to adopt children, teach school, serve in the military, or be religious professionals. Why not? Because they think we are likely to be sexual predators who will corrupt children, disrupt military order, or exploit vulnerable parishioners (which never could occur with heterosexual clergy, of course).

So the bizarre lie takes hold and becomes embedded in the

thinking of people who may oppose discrimination but who practice it without awareness. This is an important part of the challenge we face: to appeal to the decency in ordinary Americans to lift the curtain of prejudice that obscures their view of who we are.

The most effective way for any of us to meet this challenge is by simply being open and honest about our lives, sharing our reality with those we care about and want to care about us. Giving these folks a chance to balance the bizarre lie with rational truth is assuming responsibility for shaping two things: our own relationship with them and their perception of any gay or lesbian person they might ever encounter.

Unfortunately, we cannot always control outcomes, but we have a much better chance of achieving understanding and acceptance if we speak to the issue than if we opt out of the opportunities to do so. Of course, we all wish we could predict the future, find answers to the questions we have in order to decide which path to take.

For instance, we wonder what will be the direction of the movement for gay and lesbian rights in years to come. You may wonder what will happen to you as you become an active participant in that movement, if only as a fighter against bigotry in your own life. Will the payoff be worth the required effort— transcending fear, rising above inhibitions, risking the status quo, trying on new behaviors?

Will you be strengthened inside by the experience of affirming your right to be treated with respect and dignity? I believe all of this will happen to you because it has happened to everyone I know who has made the leap of faith into activism, at any level. It has happened to me, and it is still happening.

The gentle victories and quiet breakthroughs of people like you are at the core of moving the gay and lesbian cause forward, day after day, year after year, slowly, purposefully, relentlessly. Once you have stood up to prejudice and discrimination, no one can take away the exuberant feeling that produces. It becomes part of who you are, a coming attraction of what you might be capable of in the future.

Achieving Excellence As an Openly Gay or Lesbian Person

It is worth looking at a *few* examples of our contemporaries who have broken through the myth that coming out as gay or lesbian will be ruinous to life and career. These people are models of courage, to be acknowledged and applauded for their bold moves out of the closet. They are living proof that an open life can enhance, not inhibit, career achievement.

Roberta Achtenberg—This civil rights lawyer and political activist moved into the mainstream when she was elected to the San Francisco Board of Supervisors. Always an open lesbian, she was later appointed by the president to be assistant secretary for fair housing and equal opportunity in the Department of Housing and Urban Development. She gracefully endured Senate confirmation hearings with Jesse Helms predictably fuming over the selection of "that damn lesbian" to such a high office in the government. She was confirmed.

Greg Louganis—Winner of four gold medals in Olympic diving, Greg Louganis came out publicly in 1994. Speaking in that year before the U.S. Olympic Committee, he began, "I'm proud to be standing here as an openly gay athlete." Greg was instrumental in getting the Olympic Committee of Atlanta to remove an event from antigay Cobb County, Georgia, for the 1996 Games. He speaks out now as an Olympic champion and a gay man using his celebrity in the service of gay and lesbian rights.

Martina Navratilova—Arguably one of the greatest tennis players ever, Martina Navratilova has opened her life and her lesbian relationships to public view, conveying the message that being gay is not something that needs to be hidden or disguised. Her fame, and the respect she enjoys from fans all over the world, have not been diminished by her coming out, about which she says, "We have to be visible, so that we can be seen as intelligent, giving, and loving people with moral strength, dignity, and character."

Barney Frank—Acknowledged as one of the smartest members of the United States House of Representatives, Barney Frank came out as gay in 1987, and has not lost an election since. He is a highly respected political debater and deal maker, always prepared to speak out on the gay issues that emerge in the legislative process. He has said, "It finally got to the point where I knew it would be better for me if I came out. And I was right. It was wonderfully positive for me personally."

Gerry Studds—The first openly gay man in the United States Congress, Gerry Studds came out on the floor of the House of Representatives in 1983. Representing a conservative Massachusetts congressional district, he has maintained his seat in every election since then. An eloquent speaker, he is an effective advocate for gay and lesbian rights, while also being held in high regard by his constituents and his colleagues.

k.d. lang—This singer and songwriter came out in an *Advocate* interview in 1993, confirming what many people had already gleaned from her androgynous presentation. Her popularity did not suffer at all for being an open lesbian. On the contrary, she went on to become even more successful, appealing to a diverse crossover audience.

Bruce Lehman—A Washington, D.C., lawyer, Bruce Lehman is the highest-ranking openly gay man in the United States government. Confirmed by the Senate, he was sworn in in September 1993 as assistant commerce secretary and commissioner of patents and trademarks, a powerful position because of its importance to industry in America. In newspaper and magazine profiles he speaks of being gay, and of his long-term male partner. Of his swearing-in ceremony the *New York Times* commented, "The dignity of last September's swearing-in . . . suggested that Mr. Lehman had risen above society's prejudices."

Virginia Uribe—A high school science teacher, Virginia Uribe started an on-campus support group for gay and lesbian youth in 1984, coming out as a lesbian in the process. Endorsed by the Los Angeles Unified School District, her Project Ten continues to be a model for similar programs around the country, raising the consciousness of nongay students and faculty, enhancing the self-esteem of the gay and lesbian young people involved.

Sir Ian McKellen—A renowned British actor, Sir Ian came out in protest of a homophobic law in his country. Subsequently, he became the first openly gay man to be knighted by Queen Elizabeth. Since then he has been a vocal advocate for gay rights, and a frequent performer on stage and screen in the United States. He said in an interview, "Revealing my sexuality changed me as a person. . . . It now seems commonplace among critics that I am a better actor than I used to be."

Melissa Etheridge—Already nominated four times for a Grammy (and winning one), Melissa Etheridge came out publicly as a lesbian in 1993. She has since become one of the top recording stars in the rock music field, with four platinum albums and a worldwide audience of devoted fans. In an interview she said, "My work has been more successful than it ever was before. . . . I believe that confronting the fear of coming out loosened up and freed all other aspects of my life. . . . When you stand up and say, 'This is what I am,' then good things come to you. . . . I am totally an example of that."

Tony Kushner—Winner of two Tony awards and a Pulitzer Prize, playwright Tony Kushner is now considered to be one of the great American playwrights and his epic, two-part *Angels in America* has been hailed as a theatrical masterpiece. Tony unfailingly speaks and writes as an openly gay man, exploring gay issues in his work, which plays to large and diverse audiences.

Amanda Bearse—Star of a long-running television hit series, *Married . . . With Children,* Amanda Bearse came out publicly as a lesbian in 1993, has since had her contract renewed, and continues in the role of a straight wife on the popular sitcom. She has become a visible activist in the gay and lesbian community, saying, "Acting belongs on television, not in real life. That's why I stopped acting and came out. I told people I'm a lesbian. It feels great to be open and honest."

Elton John—Candid about being gay, Elton John has come out in most of his print and television interviews in recent years. "I can't compromise my life anymore. I'm not going to," he has said. And his recordings, tours, and videos are more successful than they have ever been. Elton John devotes much of his time now to raising money to fight AIDS and antigay bigotry even as he continues to perform before sold-out audiences.

Dr. Susan Love—Acknowledged as the most famous breast cancer surgeon in the United States, Dr. Love is an open lesbian who has come out in the print and television interviews occasioned by her aggressive advocacy for a breast cancer cure. When asked how she feels about going public with her lesbianism Dr. Love says, "It really is very ordinary. My life isn't that different from anyone else's."

This is just a small sample of the many gays and lesbians, in a variety of fields, who are leading the way by being public about their sexual orientation. As they achieve excellence in their work they do so as proud gay and lesbian people. They are a living challenge to minds closed around false notions of who gay people are. These people are battling bigotry by the openness with which they live their lives. They are models of courage and of a powerful option for changing the consciousness of those who have had no reason to think beyond their antigay stereotypes.

Getting Involved—In the Workplace

Various surveys have told us that the nongay society is most favorably disposed toward the plight of gay and lesbian people when job discrimination is involved. While only 40 percent of American voters support civil rights for gays, 76 percent believe people should not be fired or discriminated against for being gay or lesbian. Building on the right to work as a notion held dear by most people, there has been growing success in efforts to improve the workplace experience for many gay people.

More than three hundred U.S. corporations include sexual orientation in their nondiscrimination policies. It should be three thousand. More than sixty companies have gay and lesbians employee groups officially recognized and often funded by the company. Of course six hundred or six thousand would be better, but the reason there are any breakthroughs at all is that individual people have taken on the responsibility in their own workplaces to bring about change.

Brian McNaught, an organizational consultant, writing in *Positively Gay*, observes that ever increasing numbers of gays are coming out to their bosses and co-workers, forming support groups, conducting gay awareness education programs, and lobbying for nondiscrimination policies and for domestic partner benefits.

Success stories, so far, include such companies as AT&T, Levi Strauss, Lotus, Ben & Jerry's ice cream, Bell Communications Research (Bellcore), U.S. West, Walt Disney World, and Xerox, IBM, Apple, Bristol-Myers, Chevron, Equitable Insurance, and the Ford Motor Company, to name a few. McNaught comments: "Some companies do it quietly, others with press releases. Nearly all of them have done what they have done because *they were asked* and because it made good economic sense."

In every case of corporate breakthrough one person started the ball rolling and others joined in. One gay or lesbian individual modeling courage and determination is often enough to catalyze others looking for an opportunity to create change.

Could you be the person who goes to management to raise the question of a nondiscrimination policy or spousal equivalent benefits? How about requesting a gay awareness education program, or organizing a gay and lesbian employee support group?

McNaught, who specializes in developing and conducting programs to deal with homophobia on the job, emphasizes the importance of educating management to what gay and lesbian employees need. In his book, *Gay Issues in the Workplace*, he offers ideas on how to go about implementing any of the above ideas. It is a hands-on guidebook useful to any gay or lesbian person willing to initiate change in his or her workplace.

In the Courts—Legal Remedies

Another place to fight antigay discrimination is in the courts, which provide a somewhat more level playing field than the political arena. That is because we now have a brigade of gay and lesbian lawyers with expertise on dealing with sexual orientation issues in the legal system. And where there are no attorneys with this experience we have an invaluable resource like the legal practice book *Sexual Orientation and the Law*, published by Clark Boardman Company of New York and edited by Roberta Achtenberg.

This volume covers such areas as family law, employment discrimination, immigration and naturalization, access to public accommodations, and the defense of public sex crimes. It provides for "novel and creative applications of the law" and "creative solutions" to the legal problems of gays and lesbians. This is a book written by lawyers for lawyers, but anyone can buy it to use or give to an attorney inexperienced with sexual orientation cases to use.

Much of the progress we have made in the gay and lesbian rights movement has come to pass because individuals have been willing to seek legal remedies for being discriminated against. Lesbian mothers no longer just accept losing custody of their children. They fight back. Employees no longer just accept termination because they are gay. Gay men no longer just accept police entrapment. Gays and lesbians in the military no longer just accept that they are banned from service. They fight back.

When problems with discrimination are in the area of employment, an excellent resource for what to do is the chapter in *Positively Gay* titled "Job Security in the Workplace: Legal Protections for Lesbians and Gay Men," by David Link and Thomas F. Coleman. Following the guidelines provided, anyone can evaluate a problematic job situation and decide what course to take. The important thing to know is that there are legal bases and remedies for dealing with unfair treatment in your life. You have only to find the right information and be willing to stand up for your rights.

In the Political Process

Those who would love to homogenize the United States wave their Stars and Stripes and sing "God Bless America" and march in July Fourth parades, and they think that is patriotism. Real patriotism is educating yourself about the issues affecting the quality of life in your country. It is about participating in the political process—knowing the candidates and what they stand for, involving yourself in election campaigns, *always voting*, communicating your opinion to elected officials—being part of an informed populace shaping the future of your community and your nation.

Because gay and lesbian people are so directly affected by much of what goes on in the political process, many *are* on top of the issues, *do* work on campaigns, and write letters and make calls to our elected officials letting them know what we need and what we expect of them. Many of the gay and lesbian people I know are superpatriots in that regard.

In the Media

Another arena that is important for gay and lesbian people to stay in touch with is that of the media. While it may not always appear so, the media *have* been responsive to the efforts of gays to affect how we are written and talked about and portrayed. One way that has happened has involved *individuals* writing to networks, print publications, advertisers, and film studios when something antigay appears or when something gay-positive is published or produced.

GLAAD (the Gay and Lesbian Alliance Against Defamation) provides information in their newsletters on the good and the bad occurring in the media and whom and where to write to about it. They make it easy, and every gay and lesbian person who cares about how we are presented to the public should become a member of GLAAD and read their newsletters.*

In the Community—In the Movement

Americans are great for organizing, and gay people are no different. We have thousands of gay and lesbian organizations to cover every conceivable aspect of our lives—a gay world well be-

*GLADD national headquarters: in Los Angeles, (213)658-6775, fax (213)658-6776; in New York, (212)807-1700, fax (212)807-1806.

yond the bars and the sexual venues of old. Many of our organizations are designed to educate the nongay society as to who we are. Within this context, opportunities to counter discrimination through participation in speakers bureaus and gay awareness training programs are plentiful.

I have known many people who have put a toe in the water of public advocacy, jumped back nervously, approached again timidly, and ended up really loving the challenge of educating the world about what it means to be gay or lesbian. Self-affirming and exhilarating, the experience of presenting one's gay or lesbian self openly is also one of the most effective gambits for achieving understanding and acceptance by the nongay society.

Gay centers all over the country have speakers bureaus that send people out to schools, churches, police and sheriff's academies, social service agencies, and community organizations such as women's groups and fraternal organizations. Just being there, speaking without apology or reticence, can go a long way toward changing the consciousness of many people who have been unwitting allies of bigotry in the past.

More and more the challenge unfolds. Gay and lesbian teenagers are demanding recognition and attention to their needs in public schools throughout the country. Will they be *our* role models now? The media are hooked on gay, portraying us provocatively, sensationally, and sometimes even accurately, but not letting the reading, viewing, and listening public easily escape us. Consequently, gay as a topic of conversation can come up in the most unexpected places. Avoiding the subject gets harder and harder to do.

As the community of open gays and lesbians grows in numbers and sophistication, the opportunities for involvement increase. You can join thousands of athletes from all over the world in highly publicized gay games competition. You can celebrate gay pride in dozens of big-city mammoth parades or in first-time small-town processions of courage.

Gay and lesbian film festivals show us to ourselves in a variety of cinematic likenesses. Gay magazines chronicle the slick side of gay and lesbian life, and provide a window into the world of gay art, theater, music, books, business, and politics.

Organizations abound offering every conceivable kind of social, educational, charitable, and recreational activity. Gay and lesbian community centers are developing as hubs of service and cultural programs. Ethnic groups organize to share experiences and work to influence racial attitudes within the gay and lesbian community. Couples get together to explore their relationships. Singles get together to explore one another. Gays and lesbians with children meet in family get-togethers.

Religious gays and lesbians create ways to worship that affirm their homosexuality rather than condemn it. International gays organize to address discrimination around the world. Archival collections pay tribute to our long-neglected history. Direct-action groups mobilize to protest and to *make* history. AIDS organizations provide education, social and legal services, food, and support groups, and some lobby for fast-track research on new drugs and treatments.

Once homosexual students at university hid their secret from faculty and peers. Now, student groups ease the coming-out process of young men and women in colleges and universities and gay studies programs offer gay and nongay students accurate information about our lives.

Business and professional societies provide a networking structure and facilitate advancements in working environments for gays and lesbians. Seniors' groups smooth the way for our elders who have passed through the incredible changes that gay life has undergone in recent decades.

The gay and lesbian world is rich with opportunities to serve and be served. One need only tap in where your interests and abilities guide you. If you are not ready for much of the above, just knowing what is happening should inform your spirit with the recognition that you are part of something very powerful—a community exploding with the energy of change.

I hope this book *has* inspired in you a readiness to become involved as an active member of the community, prepared to deal with the irrationality of discrimination whenever it intrudes upon your life.

Remember, when you take the trouble to confront someone who you suspect is stuck in a prejudiced mode, you are offering a precious gift to that individual—your willingness to engage with the person, not the prejudice.

You become the role model. You are the one in charge of the encounter. If there is openness to your reality, great, you have demonstrated the way reasonable human beings should interact. If there is not openness, you continue to be the role model—direct, honest, and in touch with the real truth.

Whatever path you take in this venture, one thought should always be with you. You are not alone. There are people you've never met, in places you've never seen, thinking and feeling exactly what you are, taking the same uneasy first steps, discovering the excitement of being in on the world changing. They are your gay and lesbian companions in this struggle. They are your family.

Appendix I

In confronting homophobia in your personal life there are certain points that can always be made.

Whenever possible you should try to:

1. Identify the other person's homophobia as the real problem between you and point out that you are the same person you were before he or she learned you were gay. It is the other person who has changed.
2. Point out the harm that can be done to innocent people, like you, by unquestioned prejudices and discriminatory acts.
3. Give specific examples of the other person's homophobic remarks or actions so he or she cannot deny the connection between his or her behavior and what you are identifying as discrimination.
4. Challenge the other person to take *personal* responsibility for his or her discriminatory attitudes and acts.
5. Identify the social dangers of bigotry, mainly the inability of bigots to understand and integrate with people who are different from them but with whom they must share the planet.
6. Counter distorted and derogatory myths about gays and lesbians with the truth.
7. Establish that people making homophobic remarks cannot take it for granted that anyone listening will agree with them.
8. Clarify that being gay is not a choice, is established early in the life cycle, and is the natural, normal way for you to be, certainly not a sickness, and nothing to cure or recover from.
9. Provide a perspective on how devastating it is for the mental

health of gays and lesbians to be silent and invisible, and how necessary it is not to cooperate with that homophobic agenda.

10. Make the proper distinction between morality and conformity, and point out how those who are antigay preach morality when they really mean conformity.

11. Correct the notion that more people are "turning gay" and explain that more gay and lesbian people are living open lives.

12. Make the distinction between the religious extremist's version of God's agenda as judgmental and punishing and the God you know as loving and compassionate.

13. Question the relevance of the Bible's two-thousand-year-old code of ethics to life today, and the irrationality of your life being judged by this code.

14. Point out that the Bible has had many translators and that later versions reflect the personal (often antigay) biases of these interpreters.

15. Zero in on the other person's preoccupation with sex whenever talking about gay or lesbian people.

16. Don't let anyone get away with the ridiculous assertion that being gay or lesbian is equatable with sadism, pedophilia, necrophilia, or bestiality.

17. Provide accurate, objective information about AIDS—what it is and what it isn't.

18. Point out that a gay person making homophobic remarks is reflecting contempt for his/her own gay self.

19. Shift the focus from how acceptable homosexuality should be to how unacceptable bigotry and discrimination are.

20. Be an advocate for those gay and lesbian people who cannot (or will not) speak for themselves.

Appendix II

For many people, just reading about prejudice and discrimination, and what to do about them, is too abstract. What is needed is something more concrete, a way to make these concepts come alive in one's own life. In order to make that happen I have designed a series of exercises as opportunities to interact with the ideas and issues presented here. These exercises can be done solo, in a small informal group session, or in a large-group all-day workshop.

For the Individual Reader

At the end of appendix II you will find ten homophobic statements. On a separate piece of paper, number from one to ten, and write a two-line response to each of these statements. When you have finished writing, read over your answers and see if you can possibly improve on them. This can become an ongoing opportunity to develop your own best responses.

For a Small Informal Group

Begin by each group member writing two-line responses to the ten statements at the end of this appendix. When everyone has finished writing, go around the group and read out loud what you wrote. When this is completed have a general discussion about what you have heard. You might want to fashion new responses from the ideas of various group members.

For an All-Day Workshop

This experience will work best with a total group of no more than twelve people if the group is self-directed. In a workshop with facilitators, there can be as many groups as there are leaders. Smaller groups (eight is the ideal size) provide the most intimate experience.

Scheduling—I suggest sessions of one and a half hours each, two in the morning and two in the afternoon, with breaks between sessions one and two in the morning and three and four in the afternoon.

Supplies—You will need plenty of paper, pens or pencils, and something for the group members to write on, like clipboards or magazines.

Morning Session Number One—Exploring Prejudice

Using the material in this book on understanding prejudice, explore your own prejudices. *Write what they are, where they came from, how they play out, and what purpose you think they might serve in your own personal life.*

For instance, one idea put forth is that prejudices are handed down from generation to generation in a family. Is this true of your family? If so, what are the particular prejudices?

Another idea is that prejudices develop when there are frustrations in your life that you can't deal with because the source of the frustration is too formidable or too hard to pin down. Such prejudices usually target a group that you can find a reason to blame for your frustration. Might this apply to you? If so, what are the frustrations? What is the group?

Also, when the human landscape around us undergoes change, we might feel threatened by people who look or behave very differently from us. We then might develop feelings of hostility toward these "different" people. Has this happened to you? If so, be specific.

When everyone has finished writing, go around the group

and read out loud what you have written, then have a general discussion.

Morning Session Number Two—How Angry Are You?

How angry are you about the way gay and lesbian people are treated? Write a letter to someone in public life who you believe has done something harmful to gay and lesbian people. Let your anger come out. You can be as harsh and critical as you want.

When everyone has finished writing, place an empty chair in the middle of the group. Group members should then read what they have written to the empty chair. You might even want to place the chair in front of each person who is reading. After everyone has had a turn, go around and have each person say how all this has made him or her feel. Then, have a general discussion about what has occurred.

Afternoon Session Number Three—Personal Experiences with Homophobia

Begin by going around the group and having each person talk about homophobic experiences he or she has had. The focus should be on:

1. Whom the experience was with,
2. When and where it happened,
3. What was said, and
4. How it felt to be involved in such a situation.

Group members should also talk about any residual feelings they have about what happened, and what they would do differently now that they have read this book.

Afternoon Session Number Four—Role-playing

Group members should form into pairs. Decide who will be Person A and Person B.

Person A in each pair should read, one by one, the first five statements listed at the end of this appendix.

Person B should respond to each one with a brief retort.

Person A should argue briefly with the responses of Person B, who may then counter with a rebuttal to these arguments.

After the first five statements, the pairs should reverse roles.

Person B should then read the statements, and Person A should respond.

Person B can give Person A a hard time now.

When all the pairs have completed the task, the whole group should reconvene and discuss what it was like to be on either end of the dialogue. Group members might want to share ideas on how to make responses more impactful.

Wrap-up

When the workshop is over, group members might take the phone number of any willing member with whom they would like to continue this process outside the group.

Statements

1. Homosexuals can only replenish their numbers by seducing, recruiting, and converting young people to be gay. Homosexuals should never be around children.
2. You have made the choice to be gay, and you could choose not to be gay if you wanted to.
3. You people are covered by the same laws as everyone else. You just want special rights and special protections.
4. I think your lifestyle is disgusting, especially those half-naked men in the parades, prancing and kissing each other in public.

5. You people keep shoving yourselves down our throats. You should keep your sex lives private, like everyone else. Just live quietly and you won't have so much trouble.

6. All gay men are obsessed with sex. They have thousands of partners and their sexual desires are out of control.

7. Homosexuals are a threat to the American family.

8. Homosexuality is a sick way of life. It's abnormal, against nature, an aberration.

9. Alcoholics and drug addicts can be cured, and so can homosexuals.

10. Homosexuality is vile and abominable, against God's law and morally depraved, according to the Bible.

Appendix III

READING LIST

Aaron, Leroy. *Prayers for Bobby. A Mother's Coming to Terms with the Suicide of Her Gay Son.* San Francisco: Harper San Francisco, 1995.

Achtenberg, Roberta, ed. *Sexual Orientation and the Law.* New York: Clark Boardman Company, 1985.

Allport, Gordon. *The Nature of Prejudice.* Cambridge, MA: Addison Wesley, 1954, 1979.

Allport, Gordon W. *The ABC's of Scapegoating.* New York: Anti-Defamation League of B'nai B'rith, 1983.

Ayers, Tess, and Paul Brown. *The Essential Guide to Lesbian and Gay Weddings.* San Francisco: Harper San Francisco, 1994.

Baird, Robert M., and Stuart E. Rosenbaum, eds. *Bigotry, Prejudice, and Hatred: Definitions, Causes, and Solutions.* Buffalo, N.Y.: Prometheus Books, 1992.

Berzon, Betty. *Permanent Partners: Building Gay and Lesbian Relationships That Last.* New York: E. P. Dutton, 1988.

Berzon, Betty, ed. *Positively Gay.* Berkeley, Calif.: Celestial Arts Press, 1992.

Blumenfeld, Warren J., ed. *Homophobia: How We All Pay the Price.* Boston: Beacon Press, 1992.

Dollard, J., L. Doob, N. E. Miller, O. H. Mowrer, and R. R. Sears. *Frustration and Aggression*. New Haven, Conn.: Yale University Press, 1939.

Friedman, Richard Elliott. *Who Wrote the Bible?* New York: Harper and Row, 1987.

Gilligan, Carol. *In a Different Voice: Psychological Theory and Women's Development*. Cambridge, Mass.: Harvard University Press, 1982.

Goldstein, Arnold P., and Marshall H. Segall, eds. *Aggression in Global Perspective*. New York: Pergamon Press, 1983.

Herek, Gregory M., and Kevin T. Berrill, eds. *Hate Crimes: Confronting Violence against Lesbians and Gay Men*. Newbury Park, Calif.: Sage Publications, 1992.

Kohlberg, Lawrence. "Stages of Moral Development as a Basis for Moral Education." In *Moral Education: Interdisciplinary Approaches*, edited by C. M. Beck, B. S. Cirttenden, and E. V. Sullivan. Toronto: University of Toronto Press, 1971.

McNaught, Brian. *Gay Issues in the Workplace*. New York: St. Martin's Press, 1993.

———*Gay Issues in the Workplace*. Video. 1993. (Available from TRB Productions, P.O. Box 2362, Boston, MA 02107.)

Pharr, Suzanne. *Homophobia: A Weapon of Sexism*. Little Rock, Ark.: Chardon Press, 1988.

Shilts, Randy. *Conduct Unbecoming: Gays and Lesbians in the U.S. Military*. New York: St. Martin's Press, 1993.

What the Bible Does . . . and Does Not Say. (This pamphlet and others on homosexuality and the Bible available from Universal Fellowship Press, MCC, 5300 Santa Monica Blvd., Los Angeles, CA 90029), 1984.

Index